Other books by
Denise Carrington-Smith

The Enigma of Evolution
and the Challenge of Chance

Outshining Darwin -
Lamark's Brilliant Idea

Journeyings - Along the Path
with Edward Bach
From Rock-Rose to Rock-Water

Lord Lucan and Lady Luck

The murder that never was

Denise Carrington-Smith

First published 2018 by
Storixus Independent Publishing
Canberra, Australia
www.storixus.com

Copyright © Denise Carrington-Smith 2018

All rights reserved.
No part of this publication may be reproduced,
stored in a retrieval system, or transmitted,
in any form or by any means, electronic or
otherwise, without the permision of the publisher.

ISBN - 9780648364030 (Paperback Edition)
ISBN - 9780648364047 (eBook Edition)

PROLOGUE

My interest in the Lucan case was aroused when, during the evening of Boxing Day, 26th December, 2017, I watched a television documentary entitled: *Lord Lucan, My Husband, The Truth.*

In some ways, it was a strange documentary. The viewer never saw the interviewer, only heard his quiet voice. When not focused upon the person of Lady Lucan, then about 70 years of age, the screen was filled with family photos, home-made film footage and the occasional 're-enactment'. Lady Lucan either looked directly at the (unseen) interviewer or directly into the camera with what was a somewhat disconcerting stare, her blink reflexes being distinctly less frequent than normal. By the time the presentation was finished, I was sure - Lady Lucan was lying.

"Lucky" may have been the pet name by which Lord Lucan was known to his friends, but it was upon his Lady that Luck smiled that night.

The Lucan's Nanny, Sandra Rivett, had been found dead. Lord Lucan was believed to have murdered her. His immediate disappearance seemed to confirm his guilt. Many books have been written about what may have happened to Lord Lucan after he disappeared. Some believe he was driven to suicide, probably by drowning himself at sea, although his body was never found, nor was any abandoned boat from which he may have jumped. No boat was reported missing, which he might have deliberately scuttled as part of his suicide mission. Others have suggested that Lucan, hiding out somewhere in the countryside, died of exposure in the cold November weather. Others believe he escaped to the Continent, and may even have made his way to Africa or India, helped by friends, who forever kept silent. There have been many reported sightings of Lord Lucan over the years. If you are interested in this ongoing mystery, you may refer to the Internet, where there is plenty of material to be found.

But this is not a book about Lucan's 'afterlife'. It is about his 'crucifixion' - by his wife, by the Court of Law at the time of the Inquest and by the Court of Public Opinion thereafter, which, aided by the media, have all proclaimed his guilt.

Lord Lucan did not kill Sandra Rivett. She and Veronica Lucan became embroiled in a 'cat fight'. Their injuries were inflicted by each other upon each other. Veronica survived. Sandra did not. Lord Lucan tried to help. I plan to show that there was no murder, there was no plot. The death of Sandra Rivett was a terrible, tragic, *tragic* accident.

PART I

Three Threads Come Together

JOHN

When, on 18th December, 1934, baby Richard John first opened his eyes to glimpse the world around him, things were looking good. The world, or, at least, the European part of it, had been through tumultuous times. The Great War had rocked the consciousness of the world, but "Never again!" had been the catch cry and, as late as 1934, that was still believed to be true. The 'Shadow' had yet to spread across Europe. The Roaring Twenties had turned out to be somewhat of a see-saw as the Charleston era gave way to the Great Depression, but that had 'been and gone'. For a few precious years, the World was at peace and prosperity was returning. But, a few months later when, using all the strength his little limbs possessed, that baby turned onto his tummy, heaved his body up onto all flours and bravely made his first, hesitant, independent movement forward, Richard was already carrying a heavy burden upon his shoulders. He had been born Lord Bingham. He may have had to wait until he had turned thirty to don the title of Earl, but he was a Lord before he had drawn his first breath.

His father was the 6th Earl of Lucan. George Patrick Bingham, known as Pat, had been born in 1898, and had done all the things expected of him as a young man. He had attended Eton, then Sandhurst Military Academy, served in the First World War with honour, being awarded the Military Cross in 1918, after which he served King and Country by being aide-de-camp to the Governor of South Africa. During the Second World War, he once again served in the Military, being colonel of the First Battalion of the Coldstreams, before retiring from active service, taking up a position in the Air Ministry. He continued his service to the Crown by becoming a member of the Yeoman of the Guard, one of those colourful men in Tudor outfits, so beloved of tourists. An honourable life, but unremarkable?

No, not quite.

In 1949, Pat had inherited the title of 6th Earl on the death of his father, upon which he took up his position in the House of Lords - as Chief Whip in the Upper House for the radical Labour Government, led by Clement Attlee. His interest in politics had been ignited when in December, 1929, he had married Kaitilin, the only child of the Honourable Edward Dawson, a Captain in the Navy. Although not now aristocrats, the family definitely moved in the right circles. Her grandfather had been the first Earl of Dartrey and her mother lady-in-waiting to Queen Mary, wife of George V. Despite, or because of this, Kait had encouraged her husband to take his family on a sharp left turn politically, supporting the short-lived minority government of Ramsay MacDonald. Throughout her life, Kait was known for her support of the underdog, which, for her, meant the British working classes in their fight against their upper class oppressors.

It seems strange to me that, the Russian Revolution with its horrendous death toll, including the slaughter of the helpless princesses, having taken place so recently, and with the death toll of the French Revolution still very much in people's minds, someone as compassionate as Kait could support the potential overthrow of yet another ruling class, when far fewer people were imprisoned, tortured or killed by the ruling classes than by the triumphant working classes run wild, yet she did, and she was not alone. Stalin was rising to the height of his power, his oppressive regime being among the most brutal and bloodthirsty known to history, yet she and her husband, Pat, were staunch supporters of both Ramsay MacDonald and Clement Attlee, and Kait was to continue supporting the Labour Party under Harold Wilson after her husband's death, despite all three of these Prime Ministers being believed by many in Britain to have been Russian 'plants'. While their eldest daughter, Jane, born two years before Richard John, also had left-wing leanings, these were not shared by the young Lord Bingham, either during his childhood or his later life.

I mention this conflict of ideological thinking, because, the more I studied the life of the young Lord Bingham, the more it seemed to me that his childhood had been one torn apart by conflict. Not the conflict of warring parents, of alcohol or drugs, of poverty or crime, no, the conflicts which tore apart the life of the young Richard, or John, as he became, were ideological in nature and operated at the personal, family, national and international level.

By the time the young Lord Bingham was two years old, the world was waking up to the very real threat posed by Hitler and the Nazi Party. Neville Chamberlain made his trip to Germany, talked peace and co-operation with Hitler and returned, waving overhead the 'Agreement' which turned out not to be worth the paper upon which it had been written. The Second World War was ideological in a way that had been no earlier war. Other peoples in the past may have claimed that their Gods had told them to conquer other people and lands, but, following the dictum of Darwin (1859/1998: 198): "let the strongest live, and the weakest die", Hitler believed that he not only had a right to conquer, to prove that the Germans were the 'strongest', the superior race, but that he had a *duty* to eliminate the weak, the sick, the deformed, for that was the way evolution progressed. Stalin, too, accepted Darwin's doctrine. There was no room for hereditary rule, or privileged aristocrats. Individuals proved their worth by succeeding where others failed, by overcoming.

The young Richard John may have known nothing about any of this, but changing world ideology was about to disrupt his young life in the most profound way.

Ruddick (pp. 22-23) recorded events thus:

> The trauma, one of many to scar his early years, was the war time separation from his parents. Following the outbreak of conflict in Europe, it was widely considered to be prudent for the children of English aristocrats, who might be prominent on the execution list during an invasion, to be evacuated. Arrangements were therefore made for the four Bingham children to be sent to a retreat in North Wales ... In due course, when the travel arrangements were complete, it was decided to evacuate the children abroad to the United States ...
>
> The children arrived in Washington, D.C., in the late summer of 1940, after sailing from Southampton to Canada with Miss Coles, and then travelling across the Canadian border. The Lucans had few connections in the United States and their early days were nervously nomadic but in September a mutual friend put them in touch with Marcia Brady Tucker, a banking heiress ...

I feel I must point out that never did the Government ever make special arrangements for the rich while ignoring the poor! The Royal Family stayed in London and they, including the King, had ration books, just like the rest of us. I am sure that many families did make private evacuation arrangements - Veronica Duncan's family, for one. The children's wanderings indicate that they had no pre-arranged destination.

Thompson (p. 77) recorded the account given by Jane, John's older sister, who, having been born in 1932, would have had quite a good memory of the event:

> It was quite normal, however, to send one's children out of London at this time, when death by bomb was a very real threat. The Binghams went first to Wales, then to Canada *en route* to America. It was a very quick decision that was made in England, and they had apparently forty-eight hours to decide, any parents, whether they would accept the berths that were available on the ship. And they sent Nanny with us ...

This account fits far better with my own recollection. By 1938, the threat of invasion by German troops sailing up the Thames Estuary, was so real, perceived to be so immanent by some Londoners, that my parents sent my sister and me away from London, in the company of our Nanny, to Basingstoke - that safe, comfortable town, so near and yet so far, which will feature in this unfolding drama. By 1939, the Invasion not having happened, we were bought back home and when war did break out, and the Government did organize a general evacuation of children from London and the threatened area of the Home Counties, my parents had given up on the idea and our family stayed in London. I was not, therefore, part of the Evacuation, but from what I later heard it went something like this.

The Government acted with extreme swiftness, 24-48 hours, or something like that. Parents wishing to participate took their children, with one small suitcase and a nametag, to one of the major railways stations, such as Paddington or Euston, where they bid a hasty and confused 'Goodbye' to the parents they knew and loved, boarded a train and made the long, several hour journey to the safety of the countryside. Those people willing to take in a child (or two), waited on the platforms and, when the train drew in, quickly selected a child, usually choosing age/sex according to the age/sex of their own children, names and addresses being noted down by harassed Government officials as the train pulled away on its further journey.

But there were four Lucan children, plus a Nanny! How many ordinary households had three spare bedrooms? Not many, it seems, because no refuge was found for the Lucan children in Wales. Just pause for a moment, and consider what this experience must have been like for a frightened five year old (and there were hundreds of them), as well, of course, as thousands of others, both older and younger. Jane stated 'any parents' so she was definitely referring to the Government evacuation, not one arranged by her own parents. How many others could not find shelter? I have never heard of any Government sponsored evacuations to countries outside Britain, but Canada was part of the British family, so I suppose it might have happened. Jane wrote of berths being offered on a ship and I have to wonder whether this was a private initiative on behalf of the shipping company? Thanks to the war, they may well have had berths to spare. Whatever the circumstances, the young Binghams found themselves sailing to Canada. Just imagine their watching the shoreline of England fading into the distance, seeing the seemingly endless ocean surrounding them and then, finally, the welcoming shoreline of Canada appearing over the horizon! Well, not as welcoming as hoped, for the Lucan children found no refuge there. Next stop – America!

After finding temporary shelter in several American homes, the Lucan children were eventually rescued by Mrs. Marcia Brady Tucker, a banking heiress from one of America's most wealthy families. The Tuckers had a number of estates and the Lucan children, along with their Nanny, were provided with their own home on one of these estates, with three tennis courts and two swimming pools, one in the sun, the other in the shade (Ruddick p. 24). This was luxury beyond anything the Lucan children had ever experienced in England, aristocrat or no aristocrat. Their troubles were over! Well, I am sure Jane missed her parents. Sarah (Sally), born in 1936, may have done, at least for a while. Hugh, born 1939, would have had no memory of home back in England, but was in for a shock when he finally made it back! It was for Richard John that the troubles were just beginning.

A new born baby, if it thinks at all, thinks only of itself. As it gradually becomes aware of others, it perceives them as some sort of automaton. They become aware of facial expressions and tone of voice, but it is not until their second year that they really begin to understand that these 'creatures' which surround them have feelings. As they learn to talk, to communicate, they begin to understand 'Mummy tired', 'Mummy sad', and so on. They become aware of others around them, particularly in their own home. Up to the age of five or six, children are not truly comfortable in another house, unless it is one which they visit every day, one that feels like home. Only when the door of home closes firmly behind them, can they relax and be themselves. Richard John and his sister, Sarah, were both in this developmental stage when they were wrenched away from their home, taken here, there and everywhere for some months before finally settling with the Tuckers.

Lady Jane had progressed to the next stage, which would have had its own difficulties. At age six/seven, children become aware of other families – as real entities, not just animations. They come to understand that there are other mothers and fathers, other homes, and they start to make comparisons. This is the "My father is taller than your father" stage. It is also the 'You've got a big nose' and 'What's the matter with the colour of your skin' stage. If a comment provokes a reaction, it may be repeated the next day, and again, and again. It is the age of teasing and bullying. Children of six and seven can be as unkind as anybody of any age. Fortunately, few are yet strong enough to do much in the way of physical damage, but emotional damage to others may last a life time. Boys are generally worse than girls, so hopefully, Lady Jane did not suffer too much. But what of the young Lord Bingham?

Mrs. Tucker tried to do the right thing. She knew that upper class British boys usually went to boarding school, and so that is where she sent the poor child, yet another upheaval in his short life. She had not understood that Prep (Preparatory) School did not start in England until the age eight, nor that not all Prep School students were boarders. Some were full time boarders, if their home was in the country. Others were weekly boarders and others still were day students.

No doubt Richard John's own class mates soon simply accepted him, becoming used to his accent, but what of the boys a class or two higher? Some will have had plenty of money, others not so much, but I bet there was not one other among them with a title! John would have been an easy target for teasing, almost irresistible, in fact. Speaking to Thompson nearly seventy years later (p. 78), Jane recalled that John hated school, really hated it. He had headaches, nightmares. He tried to run away. He tried to damage things. The Brady's did their best; they sent him to a summer camp - more dislocation! They tried another school. Nothing helped.

Dealing with teasing can be hard enough for a child with a stable home. For Jane and John, torn away from their home, teasing had the potential to cause life-long psychological damage. This was not as well recognized then as it is now. Coping with teasing was seen as part of the process of growing up, of becoming tough. Crying or complaining about teasing was a sign of weakness, particularly reprehensible with boys. Children were taught to chant: "Sticks and stones may break my bones, but words will never hurt me" But they do - not physically, maybe, but the emotional scars may last a life time.

Was it just teasing, or was there more to it? Was John sexually abused as well? Yes, I think he was. It may have been older boys, it may have been a master, it may have been the gardener, who knows? But Thompson wrote (p. 79): 'I think' she [Jane] says obliquely, 'that's when it all started'. Whatever 'it' was, it obviously continued, otherwise the comment would not have been made. In 2017, a Documentary, *Lord Lucan, My Husband: The Truth*, featuring Lady Lucan was released. In it, Lady Lucan told how, when she started seeing Lord Lucan - or Lord Bingham as he then was - her friends tried to tell her that he was 'queer', which she stated was quite untrue. Did they mean homosexual or did they mean something else? Mild sexual deviance does seem to have played a role in the unfolding drama and could have been a consequence of early childhood (sexual) trauma.

Did John abandon the name 'Richard' because its 'pet' form is 'Dick'?

Be that as it may, it does seem possible that the title, which, in England, if it did anything at all, would have brought him respect, in America may have brought derision. The land which had turned its back on its Sovereign and the concept of inherited position in favour of acquired wealth, tried to bring the two together, but, for one little boy at least, it did not work!

No wonder we speak of being 'all at sixes and sevens' when we speak of being confused! The six year old has realized that all those automatons, which it sees every day in the streets and in the shops, are people. They are some other child's mother or father. And those brick buildings, with their sightless eyes, they are homes. The child is becoming aware of life outside its own home in a different way. They are beginning to choose their friends, rather than simply playing with the kid who happens to be in the same sandpit. These are the times of 'best friends today, worst enemies tomorrow' as children test each other out with acts of generosity followed, at times, with horrendous insults. Playing at another child's house without one's Mother in attendance is a big step. Gradually, confidence grows. Most people, most families, are 'O.K.' The child expands its horizons and starts to see itself as part of a community, not just a family or even a school. When people speak of 'where I grew up', it is usually the place where they were at this stage of their life which first comes to mind. So often this age is the one at which friendships are forged which have the potential to last a lifetime. John went through this stage, not only thousands of miles away from the parents and home to which he had been becoming increasingly attached, but away from his substitute home as well - at boarding school.

At last, it was time for the Lucan children to go home.

How did they fare? John had just turned ten. There would have been a wrench when he had to leave behind those first, precious, true friendships. Even worse would have been the situation of his sister Jane, older than him by more than two years. Thankfully, she was back home before the beginning of her teenage years, but she will have formed strong bonds during her time in New York. It did not surprise me to learn that, as an adult, she returned to America, married, and made her life there.

The children arrived back by boat in February, 1945. What a welcome awaited them! Their parents had written regularly, but how much had they told them? They must have been told that their house had been bombed – no one hurt, thankfully – and that they now had a new home to go to. Jane, who still remembered their old home, having been seven when she left, would probably have been the most excited to see the new place. And what a place it was! Bare floor boards. No glass in the windows – the panes had probably been removed to avoid flying glass in the event of another hit, which makes one wonder quite what the parents had experienced. John's mother is described as having worn old shoes, baggy trousers and having hair which looked as if it had come from the inside of a sofa! That sounds to me more like the 60's than the 40's, when women rarely wore trousers. We lived at Lancaster Gate during the War and had an allotment in Hyde Park. All over England, local authorities divided up strips of land where they could which people could rent to grow their own food. These were called 'allotments'. When tending our patch, my Mother wore trousers, but I remember the acute embarrassment I felt as we left our home and crossed the road into the Park. The closer we got to the allotments, the more I relaxed, but the shame of seeing my mother in trousers, I remember to this day! If John's mother really was wearing baggy trousers at that time, I'm surprised he didn't have a heart attack!

His parents did not merely vote for Clement Attlee, they embraced the 'Left Wing' Labour Party socialist doctrines with every fibre of their being. Nobody has a bad word to say about Kaitilin, who laboured tirelessly for the underdog, wherever she perceived him to be. She was outgoing, enthusiastic and, most importantly, good humoured. Kaitilin could discuss politics without making the discussion personal. She never lost a friend because of a disagreement about politics. Kaitilin was very active when it came to handing out flyers and her son (John) was to buy her a car, which he had painted red, so that she could campaign under her true colours during the Election. In England at that time, blue was the colour of the Conservative Party, green the Liberals, yellow the Labour Party and red was the colour of the Communist Party. Giving his mother a red car for campaigning was a definite message about John's thoughts on her opinions - but with humour, which seems to have been the family way. His parents were members of the local St. Marylebone Branch of the Labour Party, but with the Communist Party in Great Britain virtually defunct, the 'socialist' message had to be conveyed via the Labour Party. The last Communist member of Parliament, Benjamin Piritan, lost his seat in 1951.

The sweeping socialist programme introduced by the Attlee Government was intended to destroy the Upper Classes as thoroughly as any revolution. Iniquitous death duties had been introduced, with the intention of forcing those families owning Estates to sell. Any property in such a state of disrepair that it needed to be demolished and rebuilt automatically became State property. The intention was eventually to make all property State owned. It had the effect of introducing the biggest ever property 'mend and make do', as people rebuilt, first their dining room, then their lounge room, and so on, instead of replacing the wreck with a healthy new building, as was done in Germany, and elsewhere in Europe. How much of such work could be carried out without the building being declared 'new'? Eventually, a law was passed which declared that a building was merely 'repaired' so long as the façade remained in place. Super tax was imposed on 'unearned' income, i.e., rents and interest on investments, at £1. 0s. 6d. in every £1. Yes, it cost you money to have any investment at all. Property owners, with tenants, were unable to sell because rents were frozen at war time rates. No rent could be increased during the tenancy, which could extend for many years because all leases became 'unending'. No tenant could be evicted, even when their lease ran out. The money levied from the Upper Classes was spent on the free National Health Service the Attlee Government introduced, and which still exists in a modified form in Britain today. Public transport was nationalized. Since the train companies had been making a profit, it was assumed that this move would put money into the government coffers, but something went wrong (management!) and the trains ended up costing the tax payer millions. University education became free and all fee paying schools which received any Government assistance at all were required to offer a number of free places to children who passed the 'Eleven Plus' exam. Some working class children did receive a Grammar School education which they would not otherwise have received, but many, if not most, of the places were won by the children of parents who would have paid anyway, so the 'poor' ended up paying for the education of the 'rich' which was not a very good idea!

All of these sweeping changes (and more) were being

absorbed by a country already battered and bruised. London was a bomb site. Food rationing was more severe after the War than during it. Bread had never been rationed during the War, but it was now, making that good old stand-by, bread coated in batter and fried, more of a luxury. Scarcely a family did not know someone who had been killed or injured and even those families which welcomed back, in one piece, their 'teenage plus' sons and daughters who had been conscripted and sent overseas, still had the trauma of constant worry etched on their faces. Many returning Service people suffered terrible injuries. After school on Wednesdays, I went to Roehampton Common for my one hour weekly horse riding lesson and I remember seeing the wounded soldiers from Roehampton Hospital, enjoying the fresh air and sunshine out on the Common, from the comfort of their wheel chairs. It was terrible.

That his parents, despite their views, should have elected to send John to Eton is a mystery for which no author has even attempted to surmise a solution, but send him there they did. For a while! Then they changed their minds. They decided that Eton was incompatible with their socialist ideology and planned to send John to the local State Grammar school. (In preparation for the abolition of all private Grammar Schools, Local and County Councils were establishing Grammar Schools of their own.) John's parents had jokingly told him that if he wanted to stay at Eton, he would have to pay his own fees. It was at this point that John took charge of his life for the first time. He knew that his aunt, Christine, was leaving him money in her Will. He asked for an advance and Aunt Christine, may her soul be blessed for all Eternity, wrote him out a cheque, there and then. John was not only happy at Eton, he did well there, earning his place as House Captain of Roe's House.

After finishing school, John, like all other young, able-bodied young men, completed two years' National Service, spending at least part of his time in Germany. That would have been quite an experience. The Allies were doing everything they could to help Germany recover from the devastation she had endured. New buildings, especially new factories, were being built and Germany was fast gaining a reputation as the manufacturing centre, not only of Europe, but of the world. New technologies were becoming available and Germany's new factories were being built with this in mind. Nobody helped England recover. Far from it! England was contributing to the rebuilding of Germany. But all was not well in Germany, the country being divided into East and West. East Germany was controlled by Stalinist Russia and the capital city of Berlin, which was in the Eastern Sector, was divided. For nearly a year, June, 1948 until May, 1949, Russia blockaded West Berlin in an attempt to seize control, but the Allies organized a massive air lift of supplies, and eventually the Russians gave up and West Berlin was saved, although still divided by the infamous Berlin Wall. Stationed in Germany, so close to the Russian border, the reality of international conflict would have seemed very present to the young man, who had missed all the bombing while living in safety and luxury in America.

After he completed his National Service, John considered going to University to read English literature. In times gone by, as an 'Old Etonian', he would have had automatic entry to Oxford University, but things had changed, thanks to the Attlee government. One had to pass enough 'A' level (Advanced Level) exams to apply. Since he thought about applying, and considering he had been House Captain, I presume this would have been no problem. However, he would have had to compete with thousands of other 'A' level students who also wanted to attend Oxford. He would have had a good chance of being accepted, but, according to Ruddick (p. 27) his parents told him that he would only be able to go as an 'ordinary' student. I presume that Ruddick meant he would have to rely on the same 'Grant' as every other student. They would not be giving him an extra allowance. This would be in keeping with their attitude towards Eton. Lucan chose not to go to University.

John may have turned his back upon University, but he did not shirk study altogether, for Ruddick (p. 27) tells us that he undertook a series of banking examinations before joining the firm of Merchant Bankers, William Brandts. The photographic footage of Lucan in his twenties included in Lady Lucan's Documentary showed him to be leading a very active life, golfing, playing polo, sailing, ski-ing and, of course, racing around in his beloved motor boat. These were mostly summer activities. In the winter months, he enjoyed card games, especially those involving gambling with his friends. Those who move in the stock market and banking circles are all gamblers, of one sort or another. Some gamble with their own money; some gamble with other people's.

During the 1950's, public gambling houses were illegal in Britain. Of course, people were free to do what they liked in the privacy of their own home and John became part of a circle of friends who met regularly for cards and gambling, moving their meetings from house to house to stay within the law. Then in 1960, the law was changed. One of their group, John Aspinall, who had some private money, opened an exclusive gentlemen's gambling Club in Berkeley Square, known as Clermont. The Club was luxuriously appointed. There was an elegant dining room, with sumptuous food, in which the ladies were welcome to join their husbands for an evening meal before the men retired to the gambling area, where they stayed until the early hours of the morning, while their ladies made their lonely way home. John's nickname 'Lucky' acknowledged a particularly large win (£26,000) early in his career. Although he was never quite so fortunate again, he was good at cards and won more than he lost. He made the decision to become a professional gambler and quit his job.

The iniquitous super tax may have been no more, but tax on 'unearned' income, such as from investments, was still high. The Government did not consider gambling winnings 'unearned'. In fact, the Government did not consider gambling winnings at all. They were tax free! John's father was still alive, and it would have been he administering the family Trust Fund, along with the family accountant, but, nevertheless, John would undoubtedly have been aware of the high rates of tax being deducted from incomes 'earned' by Trust Funds and one can imagine his smug delight as he pocketed tax free winnings. As to losses – well, they were no worse than paying exorbitant tax!

Tall, dark, handsome, rich, titled – and unmarried! How did this extremely personable young man manage to reach the age of twenty-nine and still be an 'eligible bachelor'? I think the problem might have been his Mum! In those days, it was expected that the young man would call to collect his 'date' and return her safely back home at the end of the evening. Inevitably, the young man met the young lady's parents before she met his. But as the relationship progressed, the time must come for him to take her home to meet his family. Some of Lucan's lady-friends may have been titled, many probably were not, but all would have been 'ladies' as far as their upbringing was concerned. And right-wing. It was bad enough that his father was Chief Opposition Whip in the Lords, closely allied with the new Labour Party leader, Harold Wilson, but his mother!!! Not only was she an active member of the Labour Party, she dressed like a working class woman. I am sure there were now panes of glass in the windows of his home, and even some furniture on the floors, but his mother still dressed casually and her hair still looked as if it was stuffing from the sofa. How could he ask a young lady home?

Then his luck changed. He had a good friend, Bill Shand Kydd, not titled, but nicely rich. His people were 'in' wallpaper. All those houses that had been repaired and rebuilt after the war – somebody had to make money out of decorating them! This good friend had just married a lass by the name of Christina Duncan, very presentable, and she had an extremely attractive sister. Not married, very independent, busy running her own business, definitely her 'own person' with her own ideas about things, but also definitely available. Well brought up, but not aristocratic. This was someone he could take home, who would judge him for himself, not for his parents. And so it came about, that on 28th November, 1964, after a short courtship, John Bingham and Veronica Duncan were married.

The home movies which form part of Lady Lucan's Documentary show the pair, after their marriage, living 'the high life' with every appearance of luxury. His father had died two months after the wedding. Lord Lucan, as he now was, had come into money. So what went wrong?

The main problem was Veronica's mental health, which seemed to be becoming worse. John was genuinely worried about the safety of their three children. Veronica was verbally abusive, but, at times, showed a tendency towards violence, such as throwing things. No one had been hurt, but it was a concern. Veronica steadfastly denied that she had a problem and tension escalated.

Then John Aspinall sold the Clermont, which was taken over by Playboy. The Clermont had been exclusive, only 500 members, not all of whom, of course, were regular attendees. Over time, more and more of them lost more and more money and the business became less and less profitable for Aspinall. John was protected from the worst of this deteriorating situation by being a 'House Player'. This impressive aristocrat was good for business. His presence at the tables encouraged others to play. He was, in effect, playing with house money, his 'pay' being a cut of the profits. But, of course, if profits were down, his pay was down. After Playboy took over, John was no longer a House Player. It has been suggested that his increasing marital problems distracted him. He was no longer able to concentrate on his game as a professional player should – and he was drinking somewhat more, although it is never suggested that his drinking reached socially unacceptable levels.

Undoubtedly, Lucan was winning less, but that was not the only reason his financial situation was deteriorating. He had separated from his wife. He rented a 'flat', part of a house in Elizabeth Street which had been sub-divided into apartments. This accommodation was quite spacious, having five bedrooms in anticipation of his being awarded custody of the children. This was an extra expense, since he still had to support his wife and children in their home at 46 Lower Belgrave Street. Additionally, there had been a very bitter custody dispute, which he lost. Not only did he have to pay his solicitors, he had to pay his wife's legal fees as well, around £40,000. Although all three of his children were attending school, the judge, in a tacit acknowledgment of Veronica's mental instability, ordered that he employ a Nanny. Nannies want to look after babies, not stay at home all day in an almost empty house. The normal wage for a Nanny was no more than £15 per week but he was forced to pay £25.

But there was something else. In 1973, under Harold Wilson's Labour Government, England suffered a financial crisis. Oil prices rose by 70%. The stock market crashed. There were strikes. Electricity was cut off. In 1974, inflation reached 20%. There were three budgets in the one year. Obviously, the income Lucan received from the Family Trust would have been severely affected. This does not seem to have been taken into account in the literature. His failing fortunes are blamed solely upon his gambling.

When John Aspinall sold Clermont in 1972, he invested the money on the stock exchange. In the crash of 1973, he lost it all. Who's the gambler now? Aspinall probably lost more in a few days than Lucan did in a whole year. Aspinall had other money. Lucan did not. He was only entitled to an income from the Family Trust. He could not access the Trust Fund itself and the income was falling, thanks to the falling stock market and very high tax rates.

After the death of the Lucan's Nanny, Sandra Rivett, and the disappearance of John, Earl of Lucan, there was a deep division of loyalty between the supporters of Lord and Lady Lucan. Those who knew the couple almost exclusively supported John. The Police, the media, and therefore the public, were sympathetic towards Veronica, who, of course, was the only one able to tell her own tale.

Those who believed that John was totally incapable of any such violence, often cited his love for his children, saying that John spent more time with them than the average father. This is confirmed by the Nanny of the Maxwell-Scott's children at Uckfield. When the Maxwell-Scotts held weekend parties, she looked after all the children (Thompson p. 287):

> Lord Lucan ... [would] come in to the nursery — normally when they came in they'd say, This is Johnny and he's allergic to whatever and we'll see you on Sunday night. Dumped! But Lord Lucan used to come in and out, in and out.
>
> He talked to me as if I was a person. He played the piano, and so do I, and I can remember exactly, we played a duet and Frances sang it in German. He used to give me a fiver - a huge amount of money — he was the only one who did this. He would be very loving to the children. It was very noticeable, he stood out because he was very paternal.

Frances also played the piano. There was a piano in the basement apartment at No. 46. Lady Lucan cancelled Frances' lessons, so, on Wednesday, 6th November, 1974, the day before Sandra's death, rather than waste the session, Lucan took his daughter's lesson. It was to be an hour of quiet before the storm.

Lucan had three beautiful, healthy children, whom he adored. Every other aspect of his life was falling apart. He had lost his home, his wife, his children and his money. The final crash came on Thursday, 7th November, 1974, with the death of the Nanny.

VERONICA

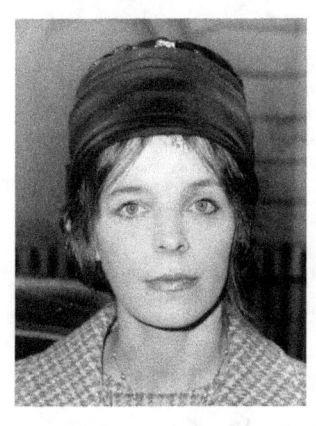

The circumstances of Veronica's early life are known in general, but details are sketchy. We are on firm ground in stating that she was born in May, 1937, at Bournemouth, now in Dorsetshire, but then in Hampshire. Her father was Major Charles Moorhouse Duncan, who was awarded the Military Cross during the First World War. His first marriage to the daughter of the 6th Baron Castlemaine, ended in divorce. His second wife, Thelma, was mother of Veronica and her younger sister, Christina, who was born mid 1939, just before the outbreak of war and just after their father had been killed in a car crash. We have no further details of Thelma Duncan. How much did the knowledge that her father had been a Major, with the Military Cross, and that his first wife was minor aristocracy, filter into the mind of the young Veronica? We do not know, but we do know that she disliked her stepfather, who does appear to have come from less noteworthy stock.

We know that the Duncan family lived for a short while in Uckfield, where John Aspinall also lived during his childhood. Aspinall was a little older, but it is possible that the two lived in Uckfield at the same time. We do not know precisely when the Duncan family moved there, or when they left. The impression is that the move to Uckfield was made after the Major's death and certainly the subsequent move to South Africa was made only by Mrs. Duncan and the children. It was in South Africa that Mrs. Duncan met and married her second husband, James Margrie. There were no further children.

We know that the family returned to England after the War but not the exact date. From 1947, Mr. Margrie ran the Wheatsheaf Inn in Basingstoke, also in Hampshire, and the town where Veronica's future Nanny, Sandra Rivett, grew up.

That Veronica hated South Africa is well recorded but the reason is somewhat obscure. Veronica apparently blamed the difficulty they experienced fitting in on their accents, although quite how much of an accent baby Christina would have had is a mute point. If they migrated to South Africa at or near the beginning of the war, Christina would hardly have been talking. Ruddick (pp. 35-36) wrote:

> In Grahamstown she and Christina were so sharply singled out, because of their accents and their late arrival into established groupings, that they were eventually removed from the school and sent to another. It was quite common, Veronica recalled, for them to return from lessons to find their beds stripped or their cupboards and drawers emptied. Veronica grew up into a pensive, highly strung teenager. The schoolgirl ragging, perhaps coupled with the loss of her father and the arrival of Margrie, made her highly competitive and over-anxious to be accepted. At one stage, she was even treated by a psychiatrist.

Ruddick fugued from pre-school to teenage with no indication as to which events occurred at which time, or even in which country. Veronica lived with her family at the

Wheatsheaf Inn in North Waltham near Basingstoke, Hampshire (as far as I know) throughout her Senior School years, so the 'stripped beds and empty cupboards' must have happened in Africa. When her parents moved to North Waltham in 1947, she was ten years old, still primary school age, although in the upper grades. The usual time for her to have started Secondary School would have been September, 1948. She attended a good school, St. Swithun's, near Winchester, the same school being attended by both her daughters. Her son, George, still Lord Bingham since his father had not yet been declared legally dead, attended Eton, fees being paid by the Family Trust. The fees for the two girls at St. Swithun's were paid by Mrs. Tucker from America. Lady Lucan contributed nothing towards the (senior) education of her three children, although why not, I do not understand, since, her husband not being legally dead, she continued to control the Lucan family finances.

Before leaving Veronica's early childhood, there are two more observations to be made. The first is that, at some point, Veronica suffered a bout of meningitis. At that time, meningitis was an extremely serious illness, with a high death rate. Veronica survived, but the illness left her 'frail'. No mention is ever made of Veronica having poor physical health at any point of her life, so it may fairly be presumed that the frailty was mental/emotional. This is confirmed by the second point. At some time during her school years, Veronica was treated by a psychiatrist. No age is given for either of these events, nor do we know how many visits she paid to the psychiatrist. We also know that she attempted suicide several times. When told that Veronica was in hospital after the attack, her sister, Christina, said: "Oh, no! Has she tried to kill herself again?"

It is to be assumed that Veronica completed her 'O'

(Ordinary) Level exams before leaving school. This would not have qualified her to apply for University but was the accepted level of education for many careers, such as nursing or teaching. Veronica attended Art School and studied graphic design. According to Ruddick (p. 36), it was 1954 when, having completed her Art course, she travelled up to London, hoping to become a model. Veronica was later to say that she would have liked to have attended University to read History "but my family didn't have the money and there were no grants" (Thompson p. 139). Sorry, Veronica, that won't wash! University was free - one of the sweeping changes brought in by the Attlee government, as previously mentioned. Students received a small living allowance. Most supplemented this with a part-time job. (Some things haven't changed!) Veronica had a tendency to play the 'poor little me' card, which was to serve her well when she needed it most - the two times she found herself in Court. No. Veronica made her choice, and it would seem to have been a good one - Art, Fashion and Interior Design.

Veronica wanted to be a model, but she was only 5 ft. 2 ins. tall. Initially, she was able to model teenage clothes, but as she grew older, this no longer became an option. Her height (or lack of it) prevented her from progressing to adult modelling. She started her own business, Resumés Ltd., printing stage scripts for the West End. Her sister, Christina, had joined her in London. Things were going well - except for one thing. Despite being very pretty, she remained unmarried. Her heart had been broken when, deeply in love, she read in the newspaper that the man of her dreams was engaged to someone else! That must have been devastating and would not have helped the mental stability of one who was already fragile.

Her meeting with John, then still Lord Bingham, was

mentioned when covering John's life. They met at a weekend gathering at the Shand Kydd's and were immediately attracted to each other. John, as always, did the right thing. He told Veronica that he was a professional gambler, explained to her what that entailed, gave her information to read on all that was involved and told her that if she could not accept his way of life, then she should not accept his proposal. Veronica even accompanied him some evenings, gambling. Nevertheless, accept his proposal she did. Three months later, they were married on 28th November, 1963. Although there were 400 guests, there were few top aristocrats present. Veronica was already antagonising John's family and friends by her argumentative nature. She was even hostile towards Kait - quite a feat, since no one else managed to have an antagonistic relationship with Kaitilin.

Two months after their marriage, John's father, Pat, died at the comparatively young age of 64. John was now Earl of Lucan and Veronica his Countess.

The home video footage shown in the Documentary is testament to the fact that, after their marriage, they were very active socially, both at home and abroad, although Veronica made it sound like a duty. In order to retain their prestige, it was important for them to be seen out and about, especially at major social events, such as Royal Ascot. When at home in London, and not otherwise socially engaged, John went gambling at Clermont. Like other wives and girl-friends, Veronica accompanied John to the Clermont, where they dined with friends and Veronica was able to enjoy a drink and a chat with other wives before wending her way home. Although, perhaps 'enjoy' is not quite the right word. Veronica was lonely. There was nothing for her at home, even after the children were born.

They were in bed, under the watchful eye of their Nanny, long before dinner was over. Veronica often stayed on, after the other wives had left, a lonely figure seated on the 'Widow's Bench'. Veronica objected to the 'all male' gambling. Wives, and other female guests, were allowed to watch, but participation was strictly an 'all male' affair. Veronica argued at the table, she argued at the 'Widow's Bench', not always in a genteel manner. She not only raised her voice, on one occasion she threw a glass of wine over another wife.

Things became difficult, although joy came in the person of little Lady Frances, born October, 1964, Veronica having fallen pregnant fairly quickly. It was to be another three years before, George, Lord Bingham, made an appearance in September, 1967. In the Documentary, Veronica spoke of this being a very difficult time because everybody was watching and waiting for her to produce an heir, which seemed to be the sole reason for her existence. Their family was completed by the arrival of Lady Camilla, mid 1970, a further three years later. Of course, there was a Nanny.

The first Nanny, Lilian Jenkins, was with the family for more than eight years, before Veronica fired her, much to John's annoyance. She then was employed by John as his housekeeper. Nanny Jenkins had been critical of Veronica as we learn from Veronica's own account in the Documentary. Apparently, Veronica 'sometimes' employed a temporary Nanny to cover Jenkins' days off. "Not even on my days off do you look after your own children" Veronica records Jenkins as having said. Veronica then confessed that she didn't really enjoy playing with the children. A scene showed her sitting awkwardly on a garden seat, while the children were playing on the ground. Veronica went on to explain that what she enjoyed was teaching the children: "My great pleasure was in teaching them to read and write and add up. Although it took perhaps 5 minutes a day doing it, I felt that was my one piece of useful thing that I did. But that was my interaction with them." No wonder Nanny Jenkins was not impressed!

The interviewer then suggested: "to an outsider, from what you have described in the last 5 minutes, it feels like a cold relationship [with your children]. Is that a wrong impression?" To which Veronica, after a thoughtful pause, replied: "Cold relationship? All my relationships were cold."

This was not quite true. In this same Documentary, Lady Lucan described a flirtation in which she had been involved with Lucan's close friend, Greville Howard. Pictures were shown of them, together with other friends, enjoying time on a boat on the Riviera. I will let Veronica speak in her own words:

> V. Now let's see who it is. That's Greville Howard. He's off to the left — the far left. I saw him every night at the Clermont Club when he had dinner ... and I got closer and closer, and looked forward to seeing him every day — that sort of thing — and gradually it was building up into something. We spoke on the telephone and various other things.
> Int. Would you say that you had fallen in love with him?
> V. Oh, yes! Definitely. Definitely. I mean, he was more of a human being than my husband.
> Int. Is that partly what attracted you to him?
> V. Partly. Probably. Anyway, my husband begins to realize. When he warned him off, he got scared. Suddenly, he turns cold, and I'm left alone — what on earth happened?
> Int. So you just felt that you were suddenly rejected?
> V. Yes. I was bewildered, to use the word.
> Int. How far had it gone?
> V. Not to the fatal end. Actually, I hadn't been unfaithful. But I just took it too hard. I just should have been more resilient. I became very depressed because of this rejection. So I took to my bed. Now, my husband, I don't know what he thought. He took me for drive and he took me to the Priory Nursing Home.

Veronica's earlier betrayal by a man she had loved undoubtedly contributed to the deep depression into which she sunk after this second 'rejection'. Nevertheless, it was apparent that, even nearly forty years later, she had no appreciation whatsoever of how hurt John must have been to have witnessed his wife, in public, so openly enjoying the company of another man, one of his best friends to boot. She insisted that she had done nothing wrong. John was clearly very worried about her deep depression, which could well have been suicidal, but, rather than appreciating that John had done everything he could to help her, despite her behaviour, she saw his taking her to a mental care facility as part of a campaign against her to prove that she was mad.

Another segment of the Documentary showed a 'double exposure' photograph. (For the young, who do not know the meaning of 'double exposure' I will explain that, in days gone by, using old fashioned cameras, one manually moved the film forward after each exposure. If this was not done, two photos were taken on the one piece of film.) One exposure showed a boat, the other a naked female bottom.

> V. Good Lord!
> Int. It's a double exposure.
> V. Yes. One is the voyage of the Crin Beu and the other is the photograph of my bottom. I think it is an excellent bottom.
> Int. And so did your husband.
> V. He obviously did. Yes. My husband liked ... his movie camera ... But I think you could say he was a 'bottoms' man.

Veronica's pose in the photograph, arms above head, looking backwards over her shoulder, smiling coyly, showed that she was not averse to having Lucan photograph her naked. She was modelling again - but this time without clothes! The photograph also reflected Lucan's fascination with 'bottoms'. Later in the Documentary, there was another segment, which contained, I believe, the key to the solution of the whole 'mystery'. Although the Documentary was made "more than thirty years" after Sandra's death, it was not released until 5th June, 2017. The information it contained was not available, as far as I know, to earlier writers.

It began with a re-enactment of Lucan winding strapping around a thin piece of stick. Then we are shown a re-enactment of Veronica kneeling on the floor, with her hands on the seat of a chair, while Lucan delivers several blows to her buttocks - which we do not see, but which were obviously bare, because Veronica continued:

> V. But he could have hit harder. They were measured strokes. Then afterwards he would be very affectionate and look regretfully at the damage he had caused. It was only repeated twice more throughout the years.
> Int. Do you think he was doing it because he got sado-masochistic pleasure out of it?
> V. Oh, he must have got pleasure out of it because we had intercourse afterwards.

The role of sado-masochistic behaviour in this drama will be discussed further in Part III during the 'unravelling'.

Veronica's mental state continued to deteriorate. After describing the wine-throwing incident at the Clermont, Ruddick (p. 46) continued:

> She had taken to chain-smoking; a doctor had prescribed mild sedatives for her depression. She was finding it harder and harder to control herself when it came to Lucan's friends. There were scenes in the poker rooms, shocking outbursts in public.

Eventually, in January, 1973, John had had enough. He made a cursory effort to have Veronica declared 'fit' to care for the children by a doctor, who, apparently just walked in, looked at Veronica, said "She's fit", and walked out again. John packed his bag and left.

Veronica took legal action, not seeking a divorce but maintenance for herself and the children. Lucan put the matter into the hands of his solicitor, an action which Veronica, in the Documentary, described as 'childish'. "He tried to turn it into sort of war". It does seem rather extraordinary that Veronica did not, at the same time, seek to determine the custody of the children, but, apparently, she did not. John did. He obtained temporary custody of the children, pending a full hearing. After a brief, but legally necessary knock at Veronica's door to advise her of what was happening, he, accompanied by two social workers, picked up the children, who had been walking home with their Nanny. This was the start of a brutal custody battle, which John lost, but not until after fourteen days of Court hearing, during which there was much 'washing of dirty linen', albeit not in public.

Veronica was later to excuse the absence of any further suitor by saying "no respectable man would have me because of the embarrassing things about our sex life that came to light" (Thompson p. 182). Here Thompson made the comment that, as always, she threw the blame on Lucan. Apparently, there were allegations, not just of violence but of deviancy, of 'le vice anglais', which may mean either sodomy or sadism. You will recall that Veronica had been warned by friends before the engagement that Lucan was 'queer'. In the Documentary, Veronica told how, on three occasions, Lucan had indulged in the 'stick and bare bottom' routine. It would seem that Lucan's preference was the 'S' role rather than the 'M'.

Lucan was accusing her of being mentally unstable; she was accusing him of being sexually deviant! Some choice the

Judge had to make! In the end, the decision was made for him when John's solicitor advised him to withdraw. In his scathing judgment, the Judge accused Lucan of arrogance in having flouted the law by kidnapping the children, which was totally untrue, since John had obtained a Court Order. John was shattered, and genuinely worried because he, alone, was fully aware of the true state of Veronica's mind.

Here may be the appropriate place to consider John's attempts to seek treatment for his wife, and to review the legal situation in regard to medical treatment in general and mental treatment in particular which is open to someone in this situation.

Every adult has the right to choose their own medical treatment. They may refuse treatment they do not wish to receive. They may receive alternative treatment, i.e. treatment offered by a person not registered as a medical practitioner. This applies to both physical and mental treatment - with one exception. If a person has been certified insane and committed to a mental health facility, that person no longer has the right to refuse medical treatment.

In centuries gone by, each family dealt with affected family members as best they could. Doctors dealt with physical problems. Severe mental abnormalities, usually attributed to possession by demons, were dealt with by the Church by means of exorcism. When both means failed, one hears stories of women locked in the attics of large Mansions. Did marriage really send more women mad than it did men? Or did the men simply not confine themselves? For the villagers, there was always the local herbalist to whom they could turn. While men worked in the fields, women worked in the garden, growing vegetables and herbs, and in the woods, collecting mushrooms, nuts and berries.

Thus the local herbalist was nearly always female, the local physician male, and this helped to fuel the great divide between orthodox and alternative treatment, which continues to this day.

It was not until the 1790's that German physician, Samuel Hahnemann, discoverer of homœopathy, opened the first residential home for mental patients. It was a moderately sized house, intended for three or four patients, which he opened because he wanted a place where he could study these people 24/7. The idea caught on and in the 1800's dozens of asylums were opened. They were horrendous places. One of the ways in which the physicians of those days were differentiating between their treatment and that of the village herbalist, was by the employment of metal-based remedies. Unfortunately, gold deepens depression, silver increases anxiety, antimony induces a bi-polar condition, with suicidal thoughts during the down times, and as for mercury, well, all those terrible mental symptoms, the 'madness' which was thought to be the third and final stage of syphilis, those are now known to have been nothing but the third and final stage of mercury poisoning. Once committed, and forced to swallow whatever medicines the doctor thought fit, it is little wonder that few who entered ever came out.

There were padded cells and strait jackets. As medical treatment changed with the dawning of the 20th century, heroic medicines were replaced with electric shock treatment, not exactly something to which anybody looked forward! After the Second World War, the world changed, and so did mental treatment. There was a far greater understanding of the problem, better testing of remedies which were prescribed far more circumspectly. Short stays became common and more and more people became voluntary patients for short periods of time. That was the option John so desperately wanted his wife to take, but she refused.

What could he do? A century earlier, he could simply have had her committed. Then, the word of the husband alone was sufficient to have a wife committed. For a man, or unmarried women, the request of a family member, plus the signature of two qualified medical practitioners, was necessary, and that is the case today for everyone. So what can a family do when the affected person refuses to acknowledge that they have a problem? Nothing, really. Unless the spouse is prepared to request that his partner be 'committed', there is nothing they can do. John does seem to have spoken to a doctor, who prescribed medication, which Veronica took, under protest, but he could not force her to take it. Today, I doubt that even that would be allowed. Both my husband and I tried to get medical help for our respective mothers when they started to exhibit symptoms of dementia, but could not. A person is responsible for their own medical care until they have been 'committed'. It can be very difficult.

Veronica swallowed lots of medication, but, apart from sedating her at night, it did not really help. John attempt to take her to a Home, without her knowledge, hoping that the staff would be able to persuade her to stay but that had not worked. Another time she agreed, but ran away on arrival. The law being what it was (and is), John's hands were tied.

In preparation for the custody case, John secretly recorded conversations with his wife, conversations in which she appeared to loose control. Veronica mentioned in the Documentary. "They were played in Court. They were more Billingsgate than Belgravia. They were awful". Billingsgate is London's Fish Market. In England, the expression "To swear like a fish wife" is to imply that the language is as bad as it can get. Here a statement made by Christina, Veronica's own sister, recalling a conversation with John, is of great importance (Thompson p. 204): "John said '... the problem about Veronica is that she is part perfectly wonderful person, but part evil.' I remember him saying evil."

In days gone by, the condition being described, the change in personality from reasonable to 'mad' or evil, was seen as being due to "possession" by another entity. When I did my psychology training, it was described as "split personality". Today, it is "dissociative disorder". Whatever it is called by the professionals, patients described it in the same way. "Something" or "someone" took over their mind and body, they lost control. It was a condition about which I was frequently consulted. Some of my patients described blackouts. They only realized when they 'came to' and they were in a different place, or had done something of which they had no recollection. No murders, thankfully, but a few reported having broken/smashed things. Uncontrollable physically destructive or verbally abusive behaviour was the main complaint. Most had perfect recollection of the event, but had no control. They were there, but as a sort of passenger. It was a very frightening and deeply distressing experience.

Of course, not all 'possessions' are by 'demons'. 'Spiritual' or 'energy' healers 'tune in', as do psychics and many writers and creative artists. I suspect performing artists do as well, although I have never heard one make the claim. However, when I watch a great pianist take his seat at the piano, pause for a moment, place his hands on the keys, and then erupt into a magnificent explosion of sound as his fingers move so quickly that my eyes cannot follow them, then I have no doubt that some other energy is at play. The difference is that the higher beings never enter uninvited, unlike the lower entities, who intrude at will. Like the earthly intruder who breaks into another person's property when he can and takes what he wishes, even if it is only the food from the fridge, these entities care nothing for anybody else, not their 'host', nor any other being. They are totally self-centred.

Over time, and the taking of many case histories, I came to notice that these patients all seemed to have suffered some form of life-threatening trauma in their early years. In one case it was a near drowning, another a difficult birth after which the person had needed to be resuscitated, and so on, but the most frequent of all was the childhood illness, with the life-threatening high temperature, from which the patient had not been expected to recover.

Veronica's meningitis and her subsequent 'frail' state!

I remember male and female patients. I think each are susceptible, although I do think loss of temper, swearing, violent behaviour are often accepted as 'normal', if regrettable, behaviour in a man, but not in a woman. Violent behaviour towards one's own family/community is not normal in any human being. We are community creatures, and community (herd/pack) mammals do not, in Nature, act violently against their own. Another pack, maybe, but not their own.

My studies of Eastern philosophy taught me that the aura, the energy field, had been damaged in the course of the trauma, which allowed undesirable entities to impinge. (Desirable ones would never dream of doing such a thing – which leaves the way open for the undesirables.) I saw my role as repairing the energy field. It worked well, although I found schizophrenia (hearing voices) harder. I spoke to a social worker who told me that she had noticed the same dissociative problems with clients who had suffered severe sexual trauma/rape in early childhood. I am glad that I am not the only person to have made this observation.

So there were two Veronicas, one who was 'wonderful' and another one who was not!

What was the 'true' Veronica like?

Veronica was very self-conscious about her size (5 ft. 2 ins.) having somehow acquired the idea that small size was associated with inferior breeding - possibly the result of some child at school having called her the runt of the litter? As she grew into adulthood, the one thing that Veronica seemed to desire more than anything was respect. She wanted to be looked up to, to be admired. Her foray into modelling well satisfied this desire, but, alas, the fullness of the dream was not realized. Veronica also joined the local theatre group and her sister, Christina, described her as a "consummate actress" (Thompson p. 139). Her business, printing scripts, kept her in touch with the theatre after she moved to London. When she married Lord Lucan, it seemed as if she had attained everything she wished for: money, title, position, best of everything - food, clothes, social life, holidays, anything she wanted, except the one thing she wanted more than anything else - recognition in her own right. It was her husband, John, who drew the attention. She was just the 'hanger-on'. Being with someone so tall (6 ft. 4 ins.) only magnified her insignificance.

Watching the Documentary, an impression is received that Veronica was totally self-centred - narcissistic. That could have been a false impression deliberately created by the producer by judicious editing. However, the same impression is gained from the books and is commented on by the authors. Everything was about her, how she felt, how she was affected by the things other people did and said about her. She never seemed to consider how her actions, or lack thereof, might have affected others. She never accepted blame for anything, and, far from being a consistent witness as claimed by Detective Gerring, she changed her story as it suited her.

An example may be taken from the Documentary. The interviewer asked her what she thought had become of Lord Lucan, to which she immediately replied that she believed he was dead, she had always believed he was dead. The interviewer politely disagreed, pointing out that in 1981 she had said she believed he was still alive. This Lady Lucan vehemently denied – until the interviewer started to show her part of a video interview she had given in 1981. She was shown sitting demurely at one end of a sofa, with a female reporter sitting at the other. Lady Lucan could clearly be heard insisting that she believed Lord Lucan still to be alive, she had always believed that he was alive. Lady Lucan quickly asked what year it was and on being told '1981', immediately waved the episode away by saying 1981 had been a very difficult year and she had been confused. It was indeed a difficult year, because it was the year in which Veronica finally lost custody of the children, who thereafter lived with the Shand Kydds.

The reason why that particular interview had been conducted in the first place would seem to have been that November 1981 marked seven years from the disappearance of Lord Lucan. If she so wished, Lady Lucan could have applied to the Courts for Lord Lucan to be declared legally 'dead'. This she was choosing not to do because, she told the interviewer, she was convinced he was alive – always had been. Other people suggested a different reason for her reticence. Once Lord Lucan was declared dead, the title would pass to her son - and so would control of the money!

Markham's book was published a further seven years later, when Lord George Bingham was turning 21, but was unable to take his seat in the House of Lords because his father had still not been declared legally dead. Being 'Countess Lucan' was one thing, being 'Dowager Countess' would have been quite another!

After the custody case, Lucan was responsible for the hiring - and firing - of the Nannies. Most seem to have left of their own accord, but he did fire one. Lucan went to extreme lengths to ensure that his children were receiving the best possible care, even hiring a firm of private detectives to keep an eye on the house and the comings and goings of the children. When he received a report that one of the Nannies had taken the children to a pub, he reported the incident to the Official Solicitor and the Nanny was fired. It turned out that she was an alcoholic, soon to be hospitalized with cancer, from which she died. She wrote a letter to Lucan: "May I say 'Thank you very sincerely' for visiting me in hospital and your gift of lovely grapes, it was most considerate of you. I did not see Lady Lucan, perhaps she was tied up with household duties." (Thompson pp. 190-191).

The only means by which those to whom Lucan had owed money at the time of his disappearance could receive settlement was by having him declared bankrupt. Lucan had sufficient realizable assets to cover his debts, the remains passed to Veronica's control, she now administering the Estate, not her son. No. 46 Lower Belgrave Street was sold and Veronica moved into the Mews house, which backed on to No. 46 and which was owned by the Trust. She would have lived rent free; her children would not have cost her much since, as already explained, their school fees were paid by others. She was a recluse, rarely rising before midday. Her needs would have been small, and yet we know that she did, in fact, sell some of the remaining assets, which were not Trust property.

Speaking to Thompson (p. 148), Jane (now Dr. Jane, married and living in America) told how Veronica had, in 2009, sold a beautiful nineteenth-century rosewood and tulipwood desk, which had belonged to her father (Pat) for £13,200. "Veronica sold some lovely things that we used to slightly weep over".

What did she need the money for? We know that Veronica used to berate John for his spendthrift ways. She wanted to put money aside for the future, whereas John seemed to take the attitude of 'enjoy it while we can' and with the various Labour Governments and the Stock Market behaving the way they did, there was certainly no guarantee that savings would still be there when needed. Lucan believed there was enough in Trust to provide for his children's education and, as for the rest, they could make their own way when they became old enough. But Veronica seems to have squirreled money away, at least during those twenty-two months when she was living apart from John, because her sister, Christina, told of her visit to St. George's Hospital the day after the attack. Asking if there was anything she could do to help, if Veronica needed anything, she said: "I mentioned money. And she said, I can assure you I've got plenty. Those were her exact words." (p. 281). From where had this 'plenty' come?

In an interview given in 1975, Veronica told how, after winning, Lucan would buy her jewellery. "I have never known anyone so generous" (p. 159). Since it was her husband who had been declared bankrupt, not her, no account would have been taken of Veronica's personal possessions. Since she spent so little, Veronica should have died a wealthy woman, but her Estate (at time of writing) has yet to receive Probate so her wealth, or lack thereof, will remain a mystery for a short time longer.

Veronica received £40 per week living expenses from Lucan but, according to Thompson (p. 193), Lucan was "running her establishment on top of his own ... All the food came from Harrods". John cancelled the account at Harrods, which he could not have done if the account had not been in his name. Veronica had a gutsy French Nanny at the time, Pierette, who 'asked' Lucan to re-instate the account, which he did. So Lucan was paying the food bills, from Harrods, no less. What was Veronica paying for? The bread and milk? The milk would have been delivered daily to the house and settled in a separate account. Perhaps she paid for the milk? Er – no! Still on p. 193, Thompson recounts:

> At the end of 1973 Lucan received a letter from Veronica's milkman: 'Your wife Lady Lucan asked me to send her account to you, but the amount of £57.62 has not been forthcoming. As we have sent several accounts, we have been forced to stop supplying. However Lady Lucan assures me on the telephone that you will pay this account directly you receive this bill.

Lucan paid. Had Lucan not paid the bill sooner because he had no money or because he considered the milk bill to be Veronica's responsibility? Milk varied in price according to its type, full cream, light, etc. Take as a round figure one shilling per pint, £1 would purchase 20 pints. Since the couple had separated in January, 1973, and this was the end of the year, it does seem that Veronica had not paid the bill for the whole of the year and that about 50 weeks' worth of milk was outstanding. She, Sandra and the children appear to have consumed about twenty pints a week! That's a lot of milk shakes! With Lucan apparently paying most of her bills, one has to wonder what Veronica did with her £40 per week. Saved it, apparently.

Do I seem to be siding with John? I must admit that the more I have read about John Lucan, the more I have liked him. Despite the luxury in which he spent the War years, he had a difficult childhood, separated from his parents for reasons which were outside the family's control, almost certainly suffering some form of physical and/or emotional abuse, followed by a difficult home-coming and an unpredictable marriage. Yet, despite, or because, of all this, he does seem to have been a very kind man.

SANDRA

In his book, *Trail of Havock*, published in 1987, Patrick Marnham told of how hurt the Hensby family had been at the Inquest that the name of Sandra Rivett had hardly been mentioned. Her father, Albert, her sister, Charmaine, and an unnamed aunt (Vera) attended every day, but the Court seemed to be more interested in Lady Lucan, her injuries and what her missing husband may have done or said to her, than they were in Sandra and what had befallen her. When they called at Lower Belgrave Street to collect Sandra's belongings, these were handed to them on the doorstep. Markham mentioned that Mr. Hensby was a factory worker, but that was it. Nothing more about Sandra as a person, only Sandra, the victim, the body.

The situation improved somewhat when James Ruddick published *Lord Lucan: What Really Happened* in 1994. Unfortunately, Ruddick obtained the information for his book mostly from Lucan's circle of family and friends and from Police Officers who had been involved in the investigation. Lucan's circle knew little about Sandra's life before she became the family Nanny and if the Police knew any personal details, they were not talking. It later turned out that some of the information given by Ruddick was wrong, although I do not blame him at all. He had been misinformed.

Ruddick, I believe correctly, described Sandra as "a kindly, attractive girl, with an even temper" (p. 67). By a coincidence of fate, she came from Basingstoke, the town near to which Veronica had grown up after the war. Sandra had married Roger Rivett, a security guard at Gatwick Airport and they had a son, who had been looked after by her parents after Sandra's marriage broke down, which had happened some eight months previously. Before working for the Lucans, Sandra had been employed as housekeeper by an elderly couple.

Ruddick suggested that the photograph of Sandra, with which we are all familiar, had been taken four years previously, when Sandra was "... rather too plump, she had flowered into an extremely attractive young woman. The hair was shoulder-length, the face had grown leaner and more sensual. In repose there was a quiet shadow of melancholy across her eyes which men found irresistible" (p. 67).

Unfortunately, we cannot judge for ourselves Sandra's sensuality or irresistibility, because Ruddick only published the usual picture of Sandra. I presume this was because he had not received permission to reproduce any others. I am also presuming that Lady Lucan had shown him pictures of Sandra and the children upon which he based part of his judgment. Who was it who told Ruddick that men found Sandra 'irresistible'? At the Inquest, Lady Lucan told the Court that, while she knew that Sandra had a current boyfriend, and had been seeing another a short time previously, she was not aware that Sandra's relationship with men was in any way other than would be expected for a woman of her age and circumstances.

Had Chief Detective Inspector David Gerring seen other photographs? Had Gerring spoken to other men who had given him that information? In 1986, a year into his research, Ruddick had travelled to an unnamed village in Kent, where Gerring, now retired, was running a pub. Gerring told of how the brewery had wanted him to call the pub *"The Vanished Earl",* but he had resisted. He had also resisted suggestions that he write a book about the case - very noble. Ruddick had particularly wanted to speak with Gerring because he was the person most actively involved in the case. Detective Chief Superintendent Roy Ranson may have been in charge, but it was Gerring who had been the person "out and about, conducting interviews, doing the experiments at Lower Belgrave Street, organizing the searches at Newhaven and elsewhere" (p. 149).

Ruddick described Gerring as 'warm' and 'charismatic'. What he did not say, possibly because he did not know, was that Gerring had not 'retired', he had been sacked for 'insubordination'! Apparently, Gerring was 'rough', and a bit of a 'red neck'. Jane would later describe him as 'louch', a term I had never heard before. I now understand it to refer to a person somewhat uncouth, a person possibly a little too fond of their drink. That could well be right.

Gerring's opinion of Lord Lucan was based as much upon his hatred of the Upper Classes as it was upon the information he was given. The more Lucan's friends and family spoke of Lucan's gentle and caring nature, the more he perceived them as a 'protective circle', who would say anything to protect one of their own. Not only was Sandra from the middle class, so, too, was Lady Lucan, despite her title. These two 'innocent' women had been taken advantage of by members of the aristocracy and the aristocracy had to pay! It was interesting that Ruddick described his feelings as he drove away from his interview with Gerring as 'confused' (p. 156).

It is to Laura Thompson that we owe a fuller understanding of Sandra Rivett. Researching *A Different Class of Murder* (2014), Thompson took the trouble to seek out Sandra's family. She spoke both to Sandra's sister, Teresa, and her son, Steven.

Born in September, 1945, little is known of the early life of Sandra Eleanor Hensby. However, one can suspect trauma of some sort at some time, because it is known that Sandra had received psychiatric help at least once during her school years. How many visits she made to the psychiatrist, and the reason for them, is not known. Nevertheless, there must have been an issue sufficiently apparent for even one visit to have been deemed necessary. That, and the fact that both women had spent time in their childhood living in Basingstoke, must have created an instant bond between Veronica and Sandra, despite the one being upper middle class and the other lower middle class, or even, possibly, working class? Ruddick had described Mr. Hensby as a factory worker; Sandra's marriage certificate stated that her father was a porter. No doubt both were correct at some time. The position of her husband, Roger Rivett, was given as 'able seaman'. Whatever her class, Sandra seems to have been well brought up, was well-mannered and presentable.

When she was eighteen, in 1963, Sandra gave birth to Steven. She named 'John Andrews, builder' as the father. Alas, being a stay-at-home Mum did not suit the temperament of the out-going, party-loving Sandra and when Steven was fourteen months old, her parents, Albert and Eunice Hensby, legally adopted him. Steven grew up believing that Sandra was his older sister. I must confess, I found this information a great relief. Ruddick had written that the baby had been born to Sandra after her short-lived marriage to Roger Rivett. I had imagined that she had deserted an infant. What was worse, she did not seem to be making any effort to bond with him when she could. There was nothing to indicate that she had spent the weekend before her death, which was her weekend off, at Basingstoke. In her telephone call to her parents in the hour before her death, she spoke of looking forward to seeing her parents at Christmas - seven weeks away! Was she not intending to visit her child before then? I was deeply troubled by this scenario.

Now I learned that Steven had been ten years old when Sandra left for London. Sandra, having been married, would not have been living with the family for some time. I doubt if he cared one iota about Sandra's move to London. It was not until two years after Sandra's death that Steven learned the truth, when he read it in a book. He was later to say that he had never forgotten the evening when two police officers arrived at his parents' caravan to tell them of Sandra's death (Thompson p. 268). Caravan! This was the first I had heard of Sandra's parents, and her son, living in a caravan. It somehow made the 'porter' and 'factory worker' more real. Remember her parents', and her son's, situation when you read, in a moment, about Sandra's flat. Oh, Sandra! Sandra!

Sandra had had a number of different jobs: apprentice hairdresser, secretary, nanny. Most interesting is that, in 1963 she had entered a mental hospital as a voluntary patient. Since no date is given, one cannot be sure, but I did note that her position as a nanny had been with a doctor and cannot but wonder if it was upon his recommendation that she became a voluntary patient? It was while in this hospital that she met Steven's father.

Three years after Steven was born, Sandra had a second baby, a boy, whom she named Gary. He was immediately given up for adoption and renamed by his new parents. Thanks to the information provided by the adoption agency in the letter given to his new parents, we know something of the circumstances surrounding his birth (Thompson p. 269):

> ... He was born February 4th [1967] and weighed 7lb. 8 oz. His mother is a single girl aged 21. She was educated at a secondary modern school and has recently been employed at a wholesale chemist ... she feels that she can't possibly bring the baby up by herself.
>
> Her baby's father is a man she has known for quite a long time but he is married to someone else. Unfortunately, while his wife had a period in hospital, she [Sandra] visited his home on a number of occasions to help in the house. Intercourse occurred and she became pregnant ...

Alas, as her sister Teresa explained to Thompson (p. 269): "Sandra was lovely with kids, but I just don't think she was cut out to have them herself".

It was a mere four months after the birth of her second child, in June 1967, that Sandra married Roger Rivett. She was still twenty-one, he twenty-two. They had no children.

Soon after their marriage, Roger Rivett was sent abroad by the navy for eleven months. Communication between the two faded, but in 1969 he left the Navy and returned to the area. Sandra took a job as a cleaner at the Reedham Orphanage, Purley, and in 1971, the couple took a flat in nearby Kenley, at a cost of £9.25 per week. At that time, an average wage would have been about £12-£15 per week.

Both were working and they had no children, so this was affordable. However, in April, 1973, Roger went abroad again and when he returned a year later, April, 1974, he moved back in with his parents. The marriage was over. Sandra went to London – but she kept the flat!

Now, why would she do that?

Perhaps a clue may be found in the picture which the police (Gerring?) found over the bed when they searched the place after Sandra's death – 'a huge colour magazine picture of a nude man' (Thompson p. 274). This was the 70's. There was no Internet. Downloading such material was not possible. Censorship laws were far more strict. Access to this type of material was not simple. Lucan's friends had told police that there were many men's names in Sandra's book, implying that she might be a prostitute, and even Gerring said Sandra had plenty of men friends and that she was receptive to their advances (Thompson p. 272).

Did Sandra return to her flat on her weekends off? And if so, why? Had Sandra experienced any sort of childhood trauma, sexual or otherwise, which contributed to the path she chose in her adult life? Almost certainly, the answer is yes. Her treatment by a psychiatrist during her school years (and later) shows definitively that some irregularity of behaviour was manifest.

The comment by her sister, that she was great with children but not cut out to be a mother may provide the answer. Teenage girls are great babysitters! Forget teddy bears and toy dolls which shut their eyes when you lie them down; here they can play with real, live baby dolls! They sing to them, read to them, play with them, and, if old enough, brush their hair, paint their nails and make up their faces. But they are always glad when the parents return home and they can hand responsibility back. Earning a bit of money to spend on clothes or going out is one thing. Quite another is giving up earning money to stay home, change nappies and spend sleepless night after sleepless night. Being awake at 1 a.m. in the morning at the local Dance Hall is very different from being awake at 1 a.m. holding a crying baby who will not go to sleep!

Sandra's happy, outgoing nature, her love of children and her hatred of responsibility, show that, emotionally, Sandra was a grown-up teenager! This type of delayed/stunted emotional development is often indicative of some type of trauma experienced at primary school age. Bearing in mind Sandra's sexual leanings, I suspect the 'trauma' was sexual. I have used inverted commas, because the experience may not necessarily have been 'traumatic'. Sandra may have been subject to grooming. This often takes place over several years and is very gentle, just a hug and a sit on the lap to start with, or even merely a 'come and sit next to me'. The perpetrators enjoy the gradualness of the strengthening bond and the friendship may never progress to any form of intercourse, just fondling – possibly by both parties. The youngster (male or female) may genuinely like the adult concerned who usually gives little treats and makes the youngster feel 'special'. If the perpetrator likes primary school aged children, they will find another victim when the first one becomes too old. Usually, part of making the child feel special is the telling them that other children may not be as grown up as they, that this behaviour is something special, 'our secret' and many people have carried this secret throughout their adulthood, possibly even to the grave.

Sandra was no street prostitute. She was not trawling street corners, climbing into the car of anyone willing to pay for her services. No! Sandra was in charge; she was enjoying herself, inviting the men she selected home for a special evening of mutual entertainment.

This was the young lady who happily swapped her position as housekeeper to an elderly couple for that of Nanny to the Lucan's three school-aged children.

PART II

Weaving a Tangled Web

Condemnation

When the not-so-young couple, John and Veronica, married in November, 1963, after having known each other only a few weeks, it was not as though they had nothing in common. Both had spent their childhood 'war years' in a foreign country and both were approaching an age when society was beginning to think of them as being 'on the shelf'. That's about it, really.

The role of women was changing fast in Post-War Britain. Before the War, few women drove, not in suburban areas, at least. There were still jokes around of the: "If a woman driver puts her hand out of the window, how do you know if she is signaling a turn or drying her nail polish?" variety. Pretty pathetic, I know, but certain people (i.e. men) found things like that amusing in those days. This despite the fact that, during the War, not only had young women (including Princess Elizabeth) driven Army vehicles, they had also driven London buses! The country's economy was a shambles. Women were doing their bit to help by continuing to work after marriage, at least until their first child was born. Some returned to work when their youngest child started school. Had Veronica married a middle class man, then she would have continued to work in her own small business, at least for a couple of years.

But she had married into the Upper Classes. Not only in Britain, nor even only in Europe, but across Asia as well, it was the unwritten rule that nobody should do a job for themselves which they could afford to pay someone else to do. Those with money were expected to share it around, not by giving it away, but by providing employment for others, so that every man had the wherewithal to support his family. Veronica, first Lady Bingham, then Lady Lucan, was supposed to join the other society ladies on various hospital and charity committees, organizing events, making speeches, raising money for good works. These activities were mostly carried out in the morning; social activities took place in the afternoon and evening. These provided work for dressmakers, hairdressers, caterers, etc. Veronica was not a social person. Working alone at her own business had suited her well and, no doubt, she had been pleased to see the profits going into her own bank account, not someone else's. Now, upon her marriage, she had been expected to give up her business and become a socialite.

Contrary to an impression which is sometimes given that all Lord Lucan's energies were directed towards his (evening) gambling activities, Ruddick (p. 28) told how surprised he had been, on going through Lucan's personal files during the course of his researches, to find how involved Lucan had still been in City activities:

> ... His papers were full of details about shares he owned in minor trading companies — from a sportswear manufacturer in the north of England, to a motor insurance agency he ran with several friends. There were numerous letters inviting him to shareholder meetings and his name appeared on the boards of directors of several company letterheads ...

It may only have been a short paragraph, but I so appreciate that Ruddick took the trouble to include it. Without it, I would have been left with the impression that

Lucan's entire time was taken up with entertainment. Now I know that Lucan did have a serious, responsible side to him. Indeed, the fact that Ruddick expressed his surprise at his find shows that I was not the only person who had formed the wrong impression.

The quick pregnancy would have brought great joy to both of them and the fact that the first baby was a girl is unlikely to have been too much of a concern. There would have been no reason not to expect another baby to have followed fairly quickly and John's own parents had had two of each, starting with a girl. John and Veronica were probably thinking that their family would develop much along the same lines. The delay between pregnancies seems to have been rather a mystery – just one of those things. Their prayers were answered when a healthy baby boy was born to them three years later. In the Documentary, Veronica spoke of how difficult this time was, of how she felt that she was being perceived as a failure until that precious boy was born. But born he was, and Veronica should have had everything she ever wanted.

Including a Nanny. I have no doubt that employing a Nanny would have given Veronica great joy. It would have been a definite 'step up' from her own childhood. The problem was that, having staff to do the work which her mother had done, Veronica was at a loss as to how to fill in her time. After the purchase of No 46 Lower Belgrave Street, Veronica put to good use her skills as an interior designer. The house was very tastefully redecorated, but, when that work was completed, what was there for her to do? Helping with the children, even caring for them on Nanny's day off, was a possibility, but not one, apparently, of which Veronica chose to avail herself. Veronica's own account of how the first Nanny criticized her for hiring a temporary Nanny to fill in on her days off, along with Veronica's estimate of the amount of time she spent each day teaching the children the 'Three R's' (five minutes) gives a good idea of her natural parenting skills. I remember, when I was studying Family Law as part of my Psychology training, reading the words of a Family Court Judge in which he said, in his experience, when a father fought for custody of the children, his concern was more with 'getting back at his wife' than it was with the welfare of the children. In the case of Veronica and John, I think the same principle was at play but the roles were reversed. Veronica had little genuine interest in the children and, once were living with the Shand Kydds, they had little interest in her.

There is no need here to repeat the account of Veronica's deteriorating mental health, of John's futile attempts to seek treatment for her, and of their final separation. Of concern now is what happened on the night of Thursday, 7th November, 1974, what were the factors which led up to the death of Sandra Rivett and what, if any, conclusions can be drawn. The Police, and the Court at the time of the Inquest, both, not only drew conclusions about what had happened, but why, and who was responsible.

There is no doubt that John was made extremely angry by the outcome of the custody case. Custody cases are held in private. Present are the couple, their solicitors and the magistrate/judge. Any information later circulated among family and friends about the proceedings, is leaked by one, or both, of the parents. Not much information has come down to us, except that a lot of negative things were said on John's part about Veronica's mental health and a lot of negative things were said on Veronica's part about John's sexual practices. Veronica, not having many friends, it may be assumed that most of the reporting came from John.

Indeed, he apparently became quite a bore on the subject of Veronica, her mental state, her care, or lack of care, of the children, details of which he shared with anyone who was prepared to listen, day after day. Scattered among his moans, groans, rants and raves, were statements such as: "I'd like to kill that woman" or: "The sooner she dies the better", not exact quotes, but words along those lines.

The much debated question was whether or not these were serious statements of intent by Lucan. Was he seriously planning to kill his wife? The Police thought so. Lucan's family and friends thought not.

The first firm evidence that John had something non-routine planned was his request to his friend, John Stoop, for the loan of his spare car. This occurred on Wednesday, 24th October, 1974. Stoop was later to say that 'he never returned it', implying that he had been under the impression that the loan was for that night or, at least, for only a short time. Stoop had told John that he would need to insure the car. Bearing in mind that John, with a few friends, ran a motor Insurance agency, that would not have been a problem, but having paid, almost certainly, for at least six months' insurance, John may have felt he was entitled to a longer period of use. Be that as it may, the car, a Ford Corsair, was still in John's possession on 7th November.

Stoop told the Police that John had needed the car that night. Furthermore, he asked Stoop not to tell anybody about the loan. Clearly, John had something planned but no one knows what that 'something' was. I believe it was, if not the first, then an early meeting with Sandra. Nobody has ever come forward with information about that Wednesday evening and the only person who could not come forward, even if she had wanted to, was Sandra.

There were reports of John being seen outside No. 46, carrying out his surveillance, but those reports were of him in the Mercedes. It was reported that on at least one such occasion he was wearing sun glasses in the car, the implication being that he was endeavouring some form of disguise. Bearing in mind John's distinctive figure, and the fact that he was sitting in his own car, this does seem somewhat unlikely. Nevertheless, all this was added to the weight of the opinion which held that John had planned to kill Veronica. Moreover, he had been planning the killing for at least two weeks. This was extremely important.

This house which John was watching so carefully, what was it like? We know of the exterior because there are plenty of pictures available. What we do not know, in precise detail, is the inside layout. From the information available, I have drawn up what I believe to have been the situation (see p. 82). On the left of the hall, there were two doors, opening into the main lounge-dining area, There was a large bay window in the front and full windows at the back, looking over the long garden. A door opened out onto a wrought iron veranda/balcony, with steps down to the garden. To the right, there was a small ante-room and cloakroom (toilet). The cloakroom now had a curtain, not a door. From the ante-room, stairs led down to the basement. These stairs were below the stairs in the hall leading up to the first floor. There was a door at the top of the basement stairs which opened outwards into the ante-room, a necessity to allow staff to open the door, while on the stairs, carrying a tray.

On the first floor, in the front of the house, there was the main bedroom, with a wrought iron balcony overlooking the Park opposite. The bathroom was '*en suite*'. There was another small room on that floor, probably intended as a study or a morning room. On the floor above was a large room, over the main bedroom, a bathroom and another smaller room. One of these rooms would have been the Nursery, the other Sandra's bedroom. Lady Frances spoke of going 'up' to the Nursery and 'down' to her parent's bedroom so we know the Nursery was on the floor above the main bedroom. There were a further two bedrooms on the next floor. George slept in the front one; the two girls shared the bedroom at the back (Ruddick p. 9). Above there was an 'attic' room, used by John as a study. Its window, apparently, had a lovely view over the Park opposite, as well as of London.

What is important to understand is that the basement was not a cellar. It was the main working area of the house, containing the kitchen, cooking and laundry areas and would have been the centre of activity during the day. Its floor area was the same as that of the main part of the house. It was partially below street level, being reached externally by steps from the street, which enabled staff to enter and leave without using the main entrance. In addition to the door, there was also a window facing the street, which, together with the back door and windows overlooking the garden, provided the basement area with ample light.

Changes would have been made to the basement with the advent of the refrigerator and washing machine, so we do not know the exact layout of No. 46 in 1974. We do know that it still retained the breakfast room (staff eating area), which was to figure prominently in the unfolding drama, and there would have been a staff toilet. Mention is made of a boiler room and we know there was a large safe somewhere. Lady Frances' piano was at the bottom of the stairs, near the breakfast room. There is no mention of a cellar, but fuel (coal and wood) must have been kept somewhere - possibly in the area next to the boiler room? What is unlikely to have been kept next to the boiler room is the wine. That needs to be kept cool and I find it hard to believe that a house in Belgravia would not have been built with a wine cellar. Since the cellar does not figure in the drama, it does not really matter.

The first indication the outside world had that something untoward had happened at No. 46 on the evening of Thursday, 7th November, 1974, was at 9.45 p.m. when a distraught and hysterical Lady Lucan ran into the pub. the *Plumbers Arms*, about thirty yards down the road. According to the publican, Mr. Whitehouse, she collapsed more or less as she entered. They lay her down and it was as she started to recover that she started shouting: "Help me! Help me! I have just escaped from being murdered! He's still in the house. My children! My children!". Lady Lucan was bloody from wounds to her scalp. The blood on her clothes was beginning to dry. The eight or nine people in the pub could not make sense of what she was saying. Instead of ringing for an ambulance, they tried to calm Lady Lucan down so that they could understand what had happened. This took several minutes with the result that it was not until nearly 10 o'clock that the Police were summoned. Police Sergeant Donald Baker, and his partner, Police Constable Phillip Beddick were in their van, making a routine cruise of the area, when they received the call to attend the *Plumbers Arms*, arriving shortly after at 10 p.m.

The two Police Officers went to No. 46. Of course, the front door was shut so they tried the basement door, which was locked. According to Ruddick (p. 8) they then let themselves in very simply by slipping a piece of plastic into the lock to release it. According to Thompson (p. 222) they kicked down the door as one of the four locks on the door had been engaged. (Later, the Police did break into Lucan's house in Elizabeth Street. Possibly, there has been confusion here?) It was dark inside and the hall light did not work. Beddick went back for a torch while Baker made his way down the hall, where he saw light coming from the cloakroom. Pulling back the curtain, he saw faint traces of blood in the basin, on the wall and on the woodwork (Ruddick p. 8). He also saw blood on the hall table, the lampshade, on the walls and ceiling. On the floor near the washroom, he noticed a small, white object, but did not pick it up.

Baker then went down the stairs towards the basement, which was also in darkness. There was a tray of broken crockery at the foot of the stairs. There was blood all over the place. Several large footprints led towards the back door. When Baker tried the door, he found it unlocked. He looked into the garden but saw nothing out of the ordinary.

Baker went upstairs to the main bedroom, where a bedside lamp was burning. He saw a blood soaked towel across the pillows. He went up to the next floor, where the two younger children were asleep, but Lady Frances was standing by her bed, anxious to know what had happened. Beddick returned with the torch and was left in charge of the children while Baker went back to the basement. First, he picked up the small, light-coloured object he had seen on the floor outside the cloakroom. It was a piece of bent piping, about 9" long, bound with surgical tape, covered in blood. In the basement, Baker found a light bulb lying on a cushioned chair in the breakfast room. He replaced the bulb in its socket, switched it on and for the first time saw the canvas mailbag in the kitchen doorway, at the bottom of the basement stairs, according, that is, to Ruddick and Thompson. According to Marnham (p. xvi), the bag was found in the adjoining breakfast room. The flap was folded over but the cord was not tied.

According to Ruddick, when Baker lifted the flap, he saw part of a human thigh, wearing black tights. He took out an arm. He could feel no pulse. Sandra Rivett was dead. Again, Marnham's account differs slightly. According to him, an arm was hanging out of the bag. I tend to believe Ruddick, because both men agree that Sandra's body had been folded over and placed in the bag head and feet first. It would have been anatomically impossible for an arm to be hanging out. A hand, maybe. An arm, no.

The Police reconstruction went something like this. Believing Sandra to be out, Thursday being her regular evening off, and knowing that his wife generally made herself a cup of tea at approximately 9 p.m., Lucan had removed the light bulb from the kitchen so that Lady Lucan would not notice his 6 ft. 4 ins. frame in the darkness, not even with the help of the light coming in through the kitchen window from the street lamp outside. (The venetian blinds were in the open position.) A small female figure came down the stairs carrying a tray with crockery. The Police surmised that Lucan attacked this woman, believing her to be his wife. Realizing his error, Lucan then went up the stairs, waited in the ante-room until Lady Lucan came downstairs. He then attacked her.

In answer to the question: "Why had not Lord Lucan simply gone up to the bedroom and attacked Lady Lucan in her bed?", the Police offered the suggestion that Lucan would not have wanted blood on the carpet and/or bedding. The kitchen had a parquet floor, which would have been much easier to clean, although he would not have been anticipating much blood. He would have expected to kill, or at least stun her, with one blow. Quite so!

Until that time, Baker and Beddick had been investigating a case of domestic violence. Lady Lucan had accused her husband, Lord Lucan of assaulting her, of trying to kill her, regrettably a situation with which Police are all too familiar, although possibly not as much in Belgravia as elsewhere. Now they were investigating a homicide. It was clear to the Police from that moment on that the same person had attacked the two women – and that person was Lord Lucan.

A report was phoned through to the local station in Gerald Road, just around the corner. Detective Sergeant Graham Forsyth was quickly in attendance. He already knew the name of the chief (only) suspect. He also knew that Lord Lucan was not at No. 46. His records told him that Lucan owned a mews cottage at nearby 5, Eaton Row, and it was there he went. Receiving no answer to his knock, Forsyth found a ladder and broke in through an upstairs window. The house was empty.

This incident is interesting for a couple of reasons. Legally, Lucan was a 'suspect'. He had not been charged. There was no warrant out for his arrest, nor did Forsyth have a search warrant. I cannot see that Forsyth had any right whatsoever forcibly to enter the premises – which, as it turned out, were rented by Greville Howard – the man with whom Lady Lucan had had her brief flirtation! Why did he break into an upper floor window, via a ladder, instead of simply breaking a ground floor window? I can only presume that Forsyth was worried that Lucan would commit suicide, and the most probable place to take sleeping pills would have been the bedroom. If Lucan had overdosed, Forsyth would have considered that there was no time to waste. There is no record of Greville registering any complaint about this intrusion, so I presume he accepted that the Police Officer acted with the best of intentions.

That Officer would later learn that there was a good reason why Greville Howard was not at home that night, He was at the theatre, with friends, watching Cole Porter. He had offered Lucan a ticket, which Lucan had declined since he had already made another arrangement. Lucan did, however, invite the theatre party to join him for dinner after the theatre, making a reservation for four people at the Clermont that night, which he did at 8.30 p.m. Greville found someone else to take the spare ticket. While the London Police Force was marshalling all its available manpower to find the missing Earl, his friends were patiently waiting for him, sitting quietly around a dinner table at the Clermont.

Would Lucan have made this arrangement for that time if he had been planning to murder his wife, and dispose of her body, that evening? On the one hand, it would have been important to be seen to maintain his usual routine. On the other hand, 11 p.m. did not leave him enough time to drive somewhere out of town to dispose of the body and be back in time. That Lucan had not made any arrangements for later that evening could be seen as supporting the 'need time to dispose of' scenario. That he did make that reservation, for that timne, could be taken as supporting the 'nothing else to do that evening' scenario. What do you think?

Extremely important was to become the testimony of the linkman at the Clermont. Fifteen minutes after making the dinner reservation, Lucan drew up outside the Clermont, speaking to the linkman without leaving the car, asking if any friends had yet arrived. The linkman replied "No" and Lucan drove off, in his Mercedes. If Lucan was seen outside the Clermont at 8.45 p.m., and the police never doubted the truthfulness of the linkman's statement, then he could not have been at No. 46 before 9 o'clock, murdering Sandra.

Either the attack took place later or it was carried out by an accomplice.

It is one of those sad 'if only' scenarios. If only Lucan had not made that other arrangement! If only Lucan had been at the theatre that night! Sandra would not have died – and nor would Lord Lucan.

More senior Officers were quickly on the scene. Detective Chief Superintendent Roy Ranson, and his assisting officer, Chief Inspector David Gerring, arrived around midnight. Knowing that Lucan was neither at No. 46 nor at Eaton Row, they went straight to Lucan's residence in Elizabeth Street. They found the Mercedes which Ruddick (p. 13) reported as having a flat battery. At this point of time, they would not have known about the Corsair, not yet having interviewed any of Lucan's friends or associates. This would have led them to believe that either Lucan was hiding with a family member or friend quite close by, or that he had fled by train and/or taxi. They did not find him. But first, they received authorization to force the front door of Elizabeth Street and to confirm that Lucan was not there. Nor, as far as they could make out, had he been. Not only was there no evidence of blood, but, carefully laid out on his bed, they found the clothes which Lucan had been planning to wear to dinner that night, along with personal possessions, such as car keys, wallet, small change, etc.

Lord Lucan's mother, the Dowager Countess, Kaitilin, was spoken to by the Police when she arrived at No. 46 to collect the children.. She had arrived at approximately 10.45 p.m., having received a phone call from her son, telling her that something terrible had happened and asking her to take care of the children. Kait did not know from which phone her son had called, but believed that it was not a public call box, since she had not heard the coins drop. Nor, apparently, was it from Lucan's Elizabeth Street house. We know that Lucan had washed his hands pretty thoroughly before he left No. 46; it seems to be possible that he could have used the phone without leaving a visible trace. However, there is evidence that there was blood on his shoe(s) which would probably have left a mark on the tile flooring of the entrance hall, which I am sure the experienced detectives would have seen, if it had been there to be seen. Despite extensive police enquiries, the telephone Lucan used has never been identified. No blood was found on any public phone within the area.

His Mother was not the only person John called that evening. First he had phoned a friend, Mrs. Madeline Floorman, who lived in Chester Square, just across the road from the *Plumbers Arms*. Even though it was still only shortly after 10 p.m., Mrs. Floorman had already retired to her bedroom and declined to answer Lord Lucan's frantic knocking on her door. A short time later, he tried ringing her. No coins were heard falling and it was subsequently assumed that this call, too, had been made from a private line. Mrs. Floorman could not understand John's incoherent pleas. Realizing that Mrs. Floorman was not going to be of any assistance, John rang off and made the call to his Mother.

By the time detectives Ranson and Gerring arrived at his home in Elizabeth Street, Lucan had already left town and was telling his tale to his good friend, Susan Maxwell-Scott, at Uckfield. As he finished his tale and prepared to leave, soon after 1 a.m., the two detectives were arriving at St. George's Hospital to interview Lady Lucan. She was somewhat groggy from the medication she had been given. Gerring (Ruddick p. 77) later said that she looked awful - blood dried on her face, tufts of hair and skin 'all over the place'. Clearly she had not yet been treated; her wounds had not yet been sutured. (I cannot here help a smile. Clearly being a Countess did not entitle her to any more speedy treatment than anyone else in the Emergency Department. Her life was not in danger, so she had to wait three-to-four hours for treatment, the same as everybody else!) Sixty stitches in all were required. The interview was brief; Lady Lucan made her statement, but there was little in the way of questioning that night – or should that be 'that morning'.

Lady Lucan had been watching television in her bedroom. The Nanny, Sandra, had offered to make her evening tea sometime after 8.30 p.m., at which time her daughter, Lady Frances, was still playing in the Nursery. A short time later, Lady Frances had come into the bedroom, asking where Sandra was. Lady Lucan had told her Sandra was making the tea. Puzzled as to why Sandra was taking so long, Lady Lucan went downstairs to find out. The basement stairs were in darkness. She called "Sandra, Sandra", then heard a sound behind her, coming from the cloakroom area. She was attacked, struck about the head and face. Her attacker tried to push her down the stairs but she managed to wrap her leg around one of the balustrades to prevent him. He then tried to throttle her by placing three (gloved) fingers down her throat. She eventually managed to place herself between his legs and grasp his genitals, upon which he let go. She realized that the attacker was her husband.

Lady Lucan explained that she had then 'talked him down', asked him where Sandra was and he had told her that Sandra had gone out. When she responded by exclaiming that Sandra would never have gone out without telling her first, John had said, simply, "She's dead". Veronica had then offered to help him, and persuaded him to take her upstairs to the bedroom so that she could lie down. Lady Frances was still in the bedroom, watching television. John had sent her to bed and then put a towel over the pillow so that she (Lady Lucan) could lie down. John then went into their bathroom to wash his hands and fetch a cloth to tend her wounds. While the tap was running, Veronica took the opportunity to escape, running down the stairs, out onto the pavement and down the road to the *Plumbers Arms*. Lady Lucan explained to the Police that she had come up with the suggestion of an 'intruder' because she feared Lord Lucan would attack her again. Her assurances that she would not implicate him in Sandra's murder, or in the attack upon her, were made to save her life. She never meant to keep the bargain. She always intended to escape at the earliest opportunity – to betray him.

Lady Lucan denied that she ever went down into the basement, a position which she was steadfastly to retain until her death nearly forty-four years later, forensic evidence to the contrary notwithstanding.

Where was Lord Lucan while all this was happening?. How did Lady Lucan's account compare with that of her husband? John had said little to his Mother on the phone, only that something terrible had happened and he needed her to go round to No. 46 to look after the children. Having ensured that his children would be cared for, he drove to the house of his friend, Ian Maxwell-Scott, in Uckfield, more than one hour's drive away, arriving at approximately 11.30 p.m. Ian had decided to stay in London that night, but his wife, Susan, took the distressed John in, gave him a drink and listened to his story. We have John's account via her testimony.

John told Susan that he was the victim of a 'terrible co-incidence'. He had been walking passed No. 46 when he witnessed a fight taking place in the basement. He let himself into the house, ran along the hall and found his wife at the top of the basement stairs, near the cloakroom, where she was being attacked by an intruder, who ran off when Lucan arrived. His wife was hysterical. It was dark in the hallway because the light was not working. (Lady Lucan explained to the Police that a number of the lights were not working because she and Sandra were too short to change them and, besides, she liked to practice economy. The Police did not know about the account at Harrods!) Because of the darkness and her distraught state, Veronica insisted that it was John who had attacked her, not who had rescued her. Lucan reassured her and took her up to her bedroom to lie down. (Their daughter, ten-year-old Lady Frances confirmed that the two of them entered the bedroom shortly after the start of the Nine O'clock News - about 9.05 p.m.)

John went into the bathroom to fetch a wet cloth to bathe her wounds. While he was in the bathroom, Veronica ran away. He heard her running down the street, yelling: "Murder! Murder!" but did not know whether she was going to tell the Police about the intruder or blame the attack upon him. In view of her previous history of belief that he wanted her dead, he feared that she would blame him. (Lady Frances confirmed hearing her father call "Veronica, Veronica. Where are you?". Coming out of her bedroom door, she leant over the bannister and saw her father come out of the Nursery, check the bathroom on that floor, run down the stairs and leave through the front door. That was the last time she ever saw him.)

There was a similarity in timing between the two stories, neither of which matched with the evidence. If Lady Frances was correct in saying that they had come back upstairs soon after 9 p.m., then clearly approximately forty minutes had elapsed before Veronica left the house and ran to the *Plumbers Arms*. Since Lord Lucan was never seen again after he left the Maxwell-Scott's house, he could not be questioned about this discrepancy. Lady Lucan amended her time line, insisting that Sandra's offer of tea was not made until just before, or even after, 9 o'clock and that they did not re-enter the bedroom until 9.25 p.m. That still meant that they were together in the bedroom for about eighteen minutes before Veronica fled.

Sometime after midnight, while still at the Maxwell-Scott's, John wrote two letters to his wife's brother-in-law, Bill Shand-Kydd, whose marriage to Veronica's sister, Christina, had precipitated his marriage to Veronica. The first letter is very sad, because it contains the first indication that John was not intending to return home any time soon. First he said that he would 'lie doggo' for a while, which could have meant anything from a couple of days to a couple of weeks - or months. That this was not what he had in mind became clear in the next sentence. "I am only concerned about the children. If you can manage it, I'd like them to live with you ... When they are old enough to understand, explain to them the dream of paranoia, and look after them." In that letter, John also wrote: "For George and Frances to go through life knowing their father had stood in the dock accused of attempted murder would be too much." The second letter was on business matters.

Some were later to argue that this was, in effect, a suicide note. Others were to argue, equally strongly, that it was not.

Since Susan had studied Law and qualified as a barrister, it is to be assumed that, after listening to John's account, Susan gave John legal advice and that advice was not very comforting. The law which forbade a wife giving testimony against her husband in Court meant that Veronica would never take the stand and would, therefore, never be cross-examined, at least as far as the death of Sandra was concerned. Veronica could testify against him in regard to the attack on her and he would find it very difficult to overturn her story, since she was injured and he was not. The same weapon having been used against both women, the extrapolation that the same person had attacked them both was almost a foregone conclusion.

For those who believed in John's guilt, a second piece of piping, found in the boot of the abandoned Corsair, the car which had been borrowed for some inexplicable reason two weeks previously, was confirmation enough, not only of guilt, but of premeditation.

Had the case come to trial, the presence of the lead piping would not have been difficult for John's defense team to explain. It was part of some game he was playing with the children. The second piece of piping would have been explained away in a similar manner. Perhaps they were planning to make a lead doll? The piece found was indeed a doll's leg and the piece in the boot was to be the body and the other leg. Head and arms to follow. Lead being malleable, the children would have been able to move the limbs and the doll (possibly a soldier) would be able to stand or sit. At the very worst, in the event that they could not convince the Court that John was not responsible for the attack, they could have argued that the confrontation had erupted spontaneously.

Why did John leave that piece of piping in the car? One can only presume it was because he forgot about it. He denied in person to Susan Maxwell-Scott that he had attacked either woman. In his letters to Shand Kydd he made no direct reference to the events at all, speaking only of an 'incredible co-incidence'. If he planned to 'lie doggo' for a while and return later to prove his innocence, removing that second piece of piping would have been essential. Everything was happening so fast; he was not thinking clearly and that piece of evidence condemned him as surely as anything spoken by Veronica.

Lucan left the Maxwell-Scott's house shortly after 1 a.m. He was seen for the last time barely four hours after Sandra's death. The last actions which we know took place occurred a further seven hours later. Within twelve hours, Lucan was gone for ever.

Susan Maxwell-Scott confirmed that Lucan had not been driving the Mercedes. The Ford Corsair was found in Newhaven Sunday afternoon. Lucan had no money with him. He had to ask Susan to stamp the two letters for him, which she did, posting them Friday morning. Bill Shand Kydd received them Saturday morning and immediately took them to the Police. Susan was interviewed, told her story, but insisted that she had no idea where John had gone when he left her place. John was known to have a boat further up the coast, but no trace of him was found there. The boat was untouched. It was thought that a friend or relative was sheltering him - he had plenty of those all over the country. Many man hours were spent interviewing and searching, to no avail. The ferries and terminals, both in England and France, were scrutinized. It was thought that he may have 'borrowed' a boat from which he had jumped overboard and drowned, but no boat was reported missing. It was thought he might be hiding on the Downs. They were searched for days, with equal lack of success. The weather being so cold, and he having no overcoat with him, his chances of survival were deemed to be slim, but no body was ever found.

It was known that John had no money with him when

he left Lower Belgravia Street. He did not ask Susan Maxwell-Scott to lend him any. His English bank accounts were untouched. If he were hiding in England, someone was supporting him. But what about overseas? He had a bank account in Switzerland. Swiss Bank Accounts are usually extremely private, but, on this occasion, permission was granted for the Police to access Lucan's account, which was untouched. The Police had to draw the same conclusion: if Lucan was alive, he was being protected by somebody.

It is known that the Corsair was parked in Newhaven between 5 a.m. and 8 a.m. The man in the house opposite got up about 5 a.m. to visit the toilet and was certain the car was not parked there then. When he got up at 8 a.m., it was. While in the car, Lucan had used notepaper in the glove compartment to write to Michael Stoop, the owner of the car. Having no money, he had to post the letter 'unfranked'. This caused a delay in delivery. Clearly, he could not remember Stoop's address, because the letter was sent to another Club, St. James, arriving Monday afternoon. By then, the Corsair had been found, so the letter did not help the Police. However, it did confirm John's state of mind. It included the words: "... if you come across my children, which I hope you will - please tell them that you knew me and that all I cared about was them." The use of the past tense is particularly poignant.

Lucan may have disappeared from sight, but he most certainly had not disappeared from mind.

There were reported sightings of Lord Lucan from all over the world. Some were genuine cases of mistaken identity; others were mischievous false alarms by people with an interest in keeping the story going. The Police searched and questioned (both people and their answers!). Gerring (Ruddick p. 76) remembered the scene as being

Photo of Outside of 42 Lower Belgrave Street

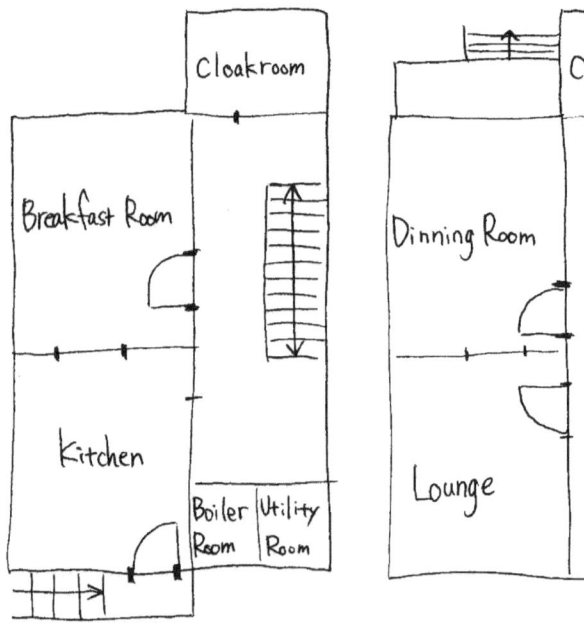

Estimated floorplan of Basement of house

Estimated floor plan of ground floor house

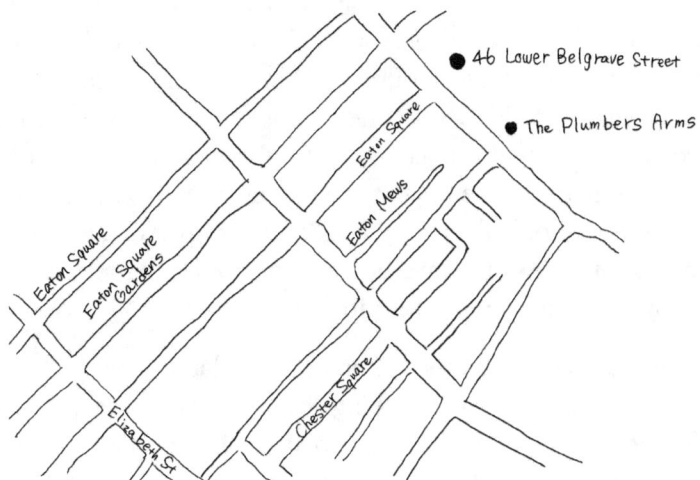

Map of Lower Belgravia area showing house loction and surrounds

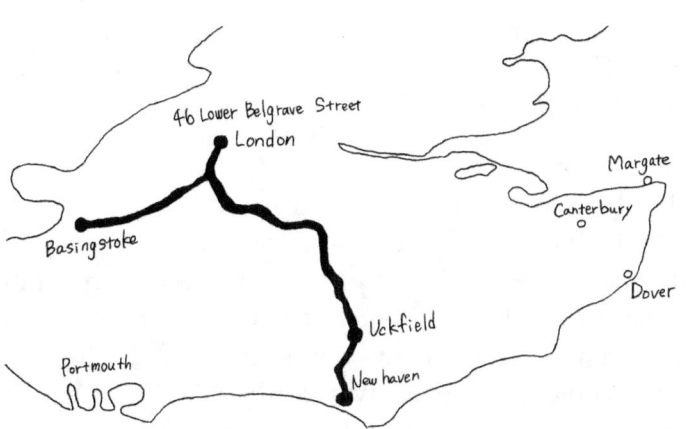

Map of Southern England showing last known locations Lord Lucan

chaotic. Had Sandra been but yet another victim of domestic violence, I doubt there would have been more than three or four officers on the scene, but Gerring reported "thirty or forty officers walking around". There seems to have been little attempt to preserve the crime scene, which was to serve Veronica well, since her blood being found where it had no right to be (i.e. in the basement) was easily explained as 'contamination'. Even the cats were suggesting as having been responsible for some of the cross contamination! There were also, of course, photographers.

Gerring, who, it was acknowledged later, had a decided bias in favour of the working classes, or, perhaps, what could more accurately be described as an antipathy towards the aristocracy, set up a 'command centre' - in Lord Lucan's house in Elizabeth Street! Here the Officers made themselves at home in Lucan's kitchen, ate his food, drank his drink and 'borrowed' his exercise bike.

The forensics team studied blood, hair and fibre evidence; the pathologist prepared his report for the Coroner. The next step should have been the Inquest. And it was! Eventually!

The Coroner delayed the Inquest, hoping against hope that Lord Lucan would be found, preferably alive. It finally started on Monday, 16th June, 1975. Despite (or because of) all the time and effort which had been put into the preparations for these proceedings, the Inquest was a complete and utter disaster from start to finish. Nor is that merely the opinion of some author or other. Was it that the Law had been poorly applied or was it that the Law, itself was poor? Wherever the blame should justly be apportioned, the Law was afterwards changed so that there would never, ever, be a repeat of what happened at that 'trial'.

Trial? Was not this an Inquest? Was not the only purpose of the proceedings to establish the cause of Sandra Rivett's death? Well, no, it wasn't, actually.

Even though they were not 'trials' as we, the public, understand the term, with a person standing accused of a crime and twelve people, good and true, deciding that person's guilt or innocence, the proceedings took place in front of a jury of twelve, whose role it was to determine whether the death had been 'accidental' or caused maliciously. It was not the Coroner who decided. Like a Judge in a criminal trial, his role was to control the proceedings, call the witnesses, ensure that the legal representatives adhered to the rules relating to the evidence which was permitted to be placed before the Court and what line of questioning could, or could not, be used.

Because nobody was ever charged, the case never became *sub judicé*. Journalists (and authors!) were free, not only to report the facts, but to speculate and comment. In a famous article, published in the *Sunday Times* Magazine the week before the Inquest, journalist James Fox did just that. Although he did point out that Lady Lucan had received psychiatric treatment before her marriage, the article was nevertheless seen to be anti-Lucan. It intimated that he was cold and uncaring, trying to encourage people in the belief that his wife was mad. Fox was an 'Old Etonian' and many of Lucan's friends had granted him an interview, expecting that the article would be favourable towards Lucan. They felt betrayed, but the damage was done. It is said that a picture speaks a thousand words, and this article was accompanied by a picture. One of the Clermont set, Dominick Elwes, dabbled in painting. For the princely sum of £200, he painted a picture of the Clermont set at the gambling table – in caricature! This did not go down well!

Also included in the article were some photographs of the Lucans, nothing disrespectful, but clearly taken from somebody's private photo album. Elwes denied that he had supplied them. Both the *Sunday Times* and James Fox supported his denials, but they did not name their source, so nobody believed them. Elwes lost most of his friends. He went overseas for a while, came back, became more and more depressed, and eventually took an overdose of sleeping pills. Yet one more tragedy!

At the Inquest, the big question was what, if anything, should Lady Lucan be allowed to say?.

As his wife, Lady Lucan could not give evidence against her husband. But her husband was not on trial. He had not been charged. Could she give evidence against her husband if he had not been accused? Well, yes, the Coroner decided, under some circumstances. It might be thought that, in relation to Sandra's death, the only evidence which Lady Lucan could give would be that of time. When she last saw Sandra alive. However, under English Law at that time, a Coroner's jury could, if they deemed it justified, not only declare the cause of death, but, in a case of murder, they could name the person they thought responsible. Whether or not they did was the decision of the jury. They were not required to do so.

Can one say that, with all the forensic evidence which had been assembled, the 'prosecution' wanted Lady Lucan to give evidence about the attack upon her? Can there be a 'prosecution' if nobody has been charged, if there is no defendant? Whatever is the answer to that question, the case proceeded as if there was a defendant - in some ways. Sometimes the Coroner allowed questions which the 'other side' thought should never have been allowed. Then he prevented cross-questioning, on the grounds that, at an

Inquest, all that was allowed was the establishment of facts. No witnesses were allowed to be questioned in a way designed to discredit them. For example, the Dowager Countess, in her original statement to the Police, had given the time of her son's call as 10.45 p.m. Since she had arrived at No. 46 at around that time, obviously she had been mistaken. The Coroner allowed her to be asked about the discrepancy, which she corrected, to the best of her ability. This was not seen to be an attempt to discredit a witness, merely to establish a fact. Quite why the time of John's phone call to his mother was relevant to the cause of Sandra's death, now that was another question, and there were plenty such questions. Lady Lucan gave her evidence, in which the times of the various events differed from those which she had originally given to the Police, but she was not allowed to be questioned about that, since the Coroner deemed such a line of questioning an attempt to discredit her. Only questions which could be answered by a direct 'Yes' or 'No' were allowed and the lawyers representing – who? – found that so difficult they simply gave up.

Enough of the problems. I am sure you have the picture. The jury found that Sandra had been murdered and that she had been murdered by Lord Lucan. Never questioned, never charged, Lucan had nevertheless been convicted, at least in the Court of Public Opinion. Such was the outcry that the law was changed. Juries now confine themselves to determining the cause of death. They offer no opinion as to the possible perpetrator.

Now to the forensic evidence. That is sound, although, to some extent, open to interpretation.

At that time, there was no DNA analysis, only blood group types. Veronica was Type A, Sandra Type B. The blood in the basement almost exclusively belonged to

Sandra; the blood in the hallway almost exclusively belonged to Veronica. There was more Type A blood on the piping than Type B. Besides the blood on the floor, there were splashes on the ceiling and walls, which had been flung off the implement as it struck repeatedly, as well as on the lamp on the hall table. Type A blood was also found in the cloakroom, including splashes on the ceiling. It would seem unlikely that Veronica was hit while in the cloakroom. It is more likely that Veronica shook her head and blood was transferred from her hair. There was one very small droplet of Type A blood on the kitchen floor and another on the kitchen bench beneath the window. Since Veronica steadfastly insisted that she had never entered the basement, these two small droplets were assumed to be contamination.

On Veronica's clothing, there were three types: A, B and AB. The Type B blood was presumed to have been transferred to her clothes from those of her attacker during her struggle. The Type AB could have been blood from her attacker, which was unknown, or could have been a mixture of the two groups. The forensic pathologist could not determine which, but it did not really matter, since the presence of a third person was a 'given'. All three groupings were found in the Corsair, some on the passenger side. There was also some Type B blood on one of Veronica's shoes, variously described as being 'under the arch' and 'under the left heel' (Ruddick p. 119). The scientists agreed with Michael Eastham, a lawyer hired by the Dowager Countess to 'represent' her son, even though he was not on trial, that this may indicate that Veronica had walked through the basement. The Coroner asked if it could also have been transferred to Veronica's shoe during the struggle, to which the obvious answer was 'Yes'.

Blood samples had been taken from six areas of the bag

in which the body had been found; four were Group B, two Group A. There was a small amount of AB. The sack had not been examined in the basement but in the laboratory. It was suggested that the Type A blood was contamination from the wall as the bag was being carried up the stairs. A photographer recalled that, when the bag had been carried down the steps to the ambulance, it had been wrapped in plastic but no one could remember whether the plastic had been put around the bag while it was still in the basement or whether that had happened in the hall, after the bag had been carried up the basement stairs.

Had the case ever gone to trial, that would have been an extremely important point and I am sure the defence lawyer would have made every effort to interview every person present, in the basement or in the hall, but this was not a trial, it was an Inquest. There were no 'disclosure' rules. The prosecution was not required to disclose all its evidence to the defence before the trial, because there was no prosecution, there was no defence, there was no trial. Mr. Eastham had to do the best he could with the witnesses who were there and they did not include all the ambulance/police officers present at the scene. If it could have been shown that Veronica's blood had been transferred to the bag while it was still in the basement, Veronica's whole testimony would have been called into question. But that was not to be.

Some Type B blood was found on a few leaves in the garden. Their presence was assumed to be transfer from the shoe of a policeman, or possibly one of the cats.

An anomaly was the lack of Sandra's Type B in the bedroom. Lady Lucan's Type A blood was on the towel which John had placed over the pillow when she lay down. No other blood was found, which was strange if John was as drenched in Sandra's blood as has often been claimed.

I have already mentioned Veronica's blood and hair on the hospital pillow. Veronica's hair was found all over the place. It was found on the piping, it was found in the cloakroom, it was found on the lampshade of the lamp on the hall table. It was found in the hall where blood had trickled down the walls. It was found in the car, although there was never any suggestion that Veronica ever entered the car. It was transferred there on whatever item it was that also transferred both the Type A and Type B blood.

There is no mention of any of Sandra's hair being found anywhere, not even on the piping.

Also found all over the place - upstairs, downstairs and in my Lady's Chamber - were grey-blue woollen fibres, presumed to have come from Lucan's grey trousers. Considering that they were found in the basement, in the hall, on the towel in the *en suite*, on the piping and in the Corsair, the assumption that they came from an item of John's clothing does seem to be justified, but the only information of any value which they provided was their absence from the sack in which Sandra's body was found, leading investigator's to conclude that John had not participated in the placing of Sandra's body in the mail bag. This was one of the strongest pieces of evidence for the presence of an accomplice and led to the suggestion that John had returned to No. 46 at the time he did to pay the accomplice. It was also suggested that John was planning to place the body in the large safe, which was in the basement, and for which the accomplice would not know the code, to be disposed of later that night, after the dinner at Clermont. It was argued that the actual killer would not have realized his mistake until he heard Veronica call from the top of the stairs. He then attacked Veronica but was interrupted by

Lucan, who let himself in by the front door after having witnessed the attack in the basement when looking through the basement window. In her confusion, Veronica did not realize Lucan had saved her, not attacked her.

The difficulty with this scenario was: Why did Lucan save Veronica? Why did the accomplice run away instead of helping Lucan kill Veronica, which was what he was being paid to do? The killing of Sandra as well might have necessitated a change of plan but it would not have necessitated an abandonment of the plan.

Some people asked how it was that Sandra had been killed, while Veronica, who had been attacked by the same man, with the same weapon, did not even lose consciousness. Veronica had a one word answer: "Breeding". This was rather strange, since it was the Upper Classes, the 'well-bred', who were considered to be 'fine boned', while it was the working classes, who laboured in the fields, who were heavy build and had the strong bones.

According to the pathologist's report given at the Inquest, Sandra had no fractures. Her death had been caused by an accumulation of blood in her airways, which had come from the nose and mouth. Sandra was unconscious and, therefore, unable to cough to clear her airways. The pathologist further concluded that the blows struck with the piping had been inflicted while she was unconscious. They were in parallel, showing that Sandra had made no attempt to move her head to avoid the blows. Some had missed her head and struck her neck and shoulders. The pathologist made no suggestion as to what may have caused blood to flow from the nose and mouth.

PART III

DISENTANGLEMENT

Vindication

Reading the previous section, it will have become apparent that there were two main areas of thinking in relation to Sandra's death. The first was that Lucan was guilty, that he, himself, had killed Sandra, mistaking her for his wife. Lady Lucan, herself, claimed that it was her husband who had attacked her, and why would she lie? What advantage would it be to her to have her husband, her children's father, convicted? These people accepted Veronica's account entirely, as it evolved. If John could not have been at the house by 9 p.m., that did not mean that he was innocent. Veronica gave an earlier time originally because she had been confused. Both women being the same height, it was not as unreasonable as some of Lucan's supporters suggested for him to have mistaken Sandra for Veronica in the darkened basement. Veronica's hair was not always the same colour - sometimes she died it, sometimes she wore a wig (very fashionable at that time). With the light bulb removed, the kitchen in semi-darkness, a mistake could easily have been made.

The other line of thinking still held Lucan to be guilty but concluded that he had not been directly involved in the attack. He had paid someone else to act for him. In some ways, this made things worse, because it evidenced a degree of planning which the former scenario did not require.

However, both accounts necessitated some planning, because Lucan was presumed to have taken the weapon with him. The second piece of piping in the boot of the Corsair was the clincher.

Lucan's subsequent fleeing from the scene (and the country?) merely added to the weight of evidence against him, but was hardly needed, since Veronica's testimony and the piping in the car were all that were required to prove Lucan's guilt.

Why, then, is Lord Lucan's disappearance still referred to as a 'mystery'. Hundreds of people disappear each year; some return or are found, others are gone forever, yet their disappearance rarely attracts media attention for more than a year. An aristocrat, an Earl no less, murdering the family Nanny, now that should have been a scandal, not a mystery. Indeed, there seemed to be no mystery surrounding who was the perpetrator, or at least the instigator, of the crime. In this case, it was not the crime that was unsolved, it was the disappearance of the presumed perpetrator. Had the 'disappearee' been a commoner, would the interest have continued for so long? I doubt it.

But it was not Lord Lucan's social standing alone which kept the story alive. It was the long list of unanswered question:

>Why did Sandra offer to make Lady Lucan's tea that night?
>Why did Sandra offer to make the tea half-an-hour earlier than Lady Lucan's usual time?
>Why did Lady Lucan's and Lady Frances' time lines differ so much?
>Why was the basement in darkness?
>Why was the light bulb on the chair in the breakfast room?
>Why was there broken crockery at the bottom of the stairs?
>Why was the weapon used so small, so malleable?
>Why was there a second piece of piping in the Corsair?

> Why had Lord Lucan been so anxious to borrow the Corsair in the first place?
> Quite how did Lady Lucan manage to 'talk Lord Lucan down', making him abandon what was held to be a long-planned murder?
> Why was some of Lady Lucan's blood found on the mail bag?
> Why did Lord and Lady Lucan co-operate for a short time after the incident?
> Why did Lady Lucan not adhere to the plan which she and Lord Lucan agreed upon?
> Why did Lord Lucan write that he might be charged with attempted murder, not murder?
> Why did Lord Lucan drive to Newhaven?

Herein lies the mystery, not in the fact of Lord Lucan's escape, or the fact that he was never seen again, but in all the unanswered questions.

Looked at from a different perspective, everything falls into place.

First, let us consider the mystery of the light bulb on the cushioned chair in the breakfast room. The bulb is supposed to have been removed by the killer to make the basement apartment darker to make the killing easier. The neurotic Lady Lucan would not, it was assumed, have been deterred by the darkness. She would still have come down the stairs, crossed the floor to where the kettle was on the bench and started to make the tea by the street light coming through the open Venetian blinds of the kitchen window.

Although it is never stated, I assume that there was a staff toilet in the basement – the staff would not have come upstairs to use the 'house' facility. That would have been the place for the killer to lie in wait, if he needed to be hidden.

I do not believe the light bulb had anything to do with the death. I am going to suggest something very simple.

When Sandra prepared supper at around 5 p.m., darkness would already have fallen that November evening. It must be assumed that the light in the kitchen was working at that time. At some point later in the evening, it was removed and found on a cushioned chair in the breakfast room. I suggest Sandra was planning to use the breakfast room that evening. There being no spare bulb, she had no option but to remove the light bulb from the kitchen – the basement ceilings happily not being as high as those of the main floors, she was able to do this. She was just about to climb up onto the chair in the breakfast room to insert the bulb, when Lady Lucan called to her from the top of the stairs.

No mention is made of a spent bulb in the bin, so I assume there was none. Presumably Sandra was aware of the need to buy another bulb. Perhaps she had been planning to buy one but forgot? Lady Frances had not attended school that day. She explained that the bus had not picked her up. Apparently, Lady Lucan did not send her to school on Sandra's day off. That week, Sandra's day off had been changed to Wednesday, but if no one had thought to advise the bus driver, he would not have picked Lady Frances up that Thursday. Lucan was aware of this habit and had phoned the school that morning to ask if Frances was at school. The school office said they would check and call back, which they did, but Lucan must have been out because he did not answer the phone.

Keeping an eye on Lady Frances would have disrupted Sandra's usual routine. Lady Frances may have spent most of the day playing by herself in the Nursery, but any Nanny worth her salt would have spent some time with her. There has never been any suggestion that Sandra was not very good at her job and she would probably have found the company of Lady Frances quite a pleasant change. The only thing we know about that day is that they went out in the afternoon to post some letters. No mention is made of any trip to the shops. Sandra forgot to buy more light bulbs.

Lady Frances recalled that they had had their evening meal between 5 p.m. and 5.30 p.m. The Police obviously spoke to her on more than one occasion because authors give slightly different accounts. For example, part of the statement recorded by Ruddick (p. 19) reads:

> After tea I played with some of my games in the Nursery. Sandra brought George and Camilla up stairs and put them to bed. I stayed in the Nursery and then went downstairs to Mummy's bedroom. That would have been about 8.40 p.m.

It is this statement which makes it apparent that the Nursery was on the floor above the Lucan's bedroom. Testimony states that the two younger children watched television with their Mother in her room after supper that evening. "Sandra brought George and Camilla up stairs and put them to bed" does sound as if Lady Frances was 'upstairs' in the Nursery at that particular time. We know that she was on her own part of that evening (Marnham p, 183):

> ... At 7.20 I watched Top of the Pops on TV in the nursery. Mummy, Camilla, George and Sandra were downstairs watching The Six Million Dollar Man. I joined them at 8.05 and we all watched TV in Mummy's room. When the programme finished at 8.30 I went back to the nursery and played with my game. Sandra brought Camilla and George upstairs and put them to bed. I had had my bath and was wearing my pyjamas. I stayed in the nursery about five minutes. I went downstairs again to Mummy's room at about 8.40. I asked Mummy where Sandra was and Mummy said she was downstairs making tea.
>
> ... At 9.05 the News was on TV and Daddy and Mummy both walked into the room ...

Marnham suggested that Lady Frances' account was given from the perspective of a child whose time was determined by the television programmes. She would not have allowed for advertising. Be that as it may, it gives the impression of being the statement of a person who was very well aware of the time – as most ten-year-olds are when bed time is approaching! How I wish I knew whether Lady Frances actually said "7.20, 8.05, 8.30, 8.40 and 9.05, or whether she said "twenty past seven ...", etc., and the officer used the shorter transcription. If my memory serves me correctly, it was in the 1970's that the old style clock 'face', with 'hands' started to be replaced with far more sensible clocks – three or four large, clear digits in a straight line! Somehow, the account reads like that of a child who has the actual numbers impressed upon her brain. The only times of which she was not certain were the times her mother left the bedroom on each occasion – when she went downstairs to check on Sandra's tea making and when she left to flee the house.

At some point, all three children had their bath. Lady Frances' account makes it sound as though her mother, Sandra, George and Camilla were all together, watching television, for the whole evening, with her joining them intermittently. This was clearly not the case, since Sandra would have prepared and supervised the baths of the other two children. We also know Sandra left the room for a short time at least when she telephoned her parents. Lady Lucan also stated that Sandra did some ironing in her room.

Lady Frances stated that she had already had her bath and was ready for bed before she went back to the Nursery for a few minutes, returning to Lady Lucan's bedroom at around 8.40 p.m. During that ten minutes, Sandra had tucked both the younger children into bed, come back downstairs and popped her head around Lady Lucan's bedroom door with her offer of tea.

What Lady Frances does not tell us is her usual bedtime. Some accounts have suggested she usually continued watching television until 9 p.m., or, even, that she watched the News with her mother until 9.30 p.m. I doubt this. The Court Order stipulated that the children must be under the care of a Nanny 'at all times'. The Nanny could not be considered to be off duty until all the children were in bed. It is highly unlikely that any of the Nannies would have agreed to a 9.30 p.m. finishing time. 9 p.m. - possibly. 9.30 p.m. - no! It is possible that the Nanny went off duty at 8.30 p.m., the children's bed time. Most T.V. programmes finish a couple of minutes early. Even tucking the two younger children into bed first and then taking Lady Frances up to bed after would not have involved much 'over time'. Lord Lucan was keeping an eagle eye on everything which was happening at No. 46, watching out for any breach of the Court Order which would give him a reason/excuse to report his wife for a violation. He had even hired a detective firm, which had already discovered that one of the Nannies was an alcoholic, not only visiting the pub during working hours, but taking the children with her. The last thing Lady Lucan would have wanted was to give her husband further grounds for complaint.

If Lady Frances usually continued watching the television with her Mother, why had she gone to the Nursery for that short time? Was she expecting to find Sandra watching T.V. with Lady Lucan when she returned? If Sandra usually continued watching television with Lady Lucan, would not Sandra have made the tea just before 9 p.m., rather than Lady Lucan? There is general agreement that it was Lady Lucan's usual practice to go down to the basement just before 9 p.m. to make her own tea, which she drank while watching the News. Indeed, the whole planned murder scenario hinged on this.

For these reasons, I have concluded that the three children were usually put to bed around 8.30 p.m, the younger two first, then Lady Frances a few minutes later.

Quite how long it would have taken for Sandra to prepare the tea we cannot be certain, but no more than ten minutes would, I think, be a reasonable guess. Kettles in those days were not the 'speedy-boil' variety to which we are used today. While quicker than gas, electric kettles still took several minutes to boil. Sandra had apparently already prepared the tray, placing it on the staircase ready to take upstairs, when she made the fateful decision, which eventually cost her her life: to change the light bulb. She was expecting a visitor, whom she planned to entertain in the breakfast room. The lack of a light in the kitchen would not have been a major problem at that point. The kitchen bench was under the window and there would have been sufficient light coming through the kitchen window, especially with the blinds in the 'open' position, for her to fill the tea pot. She removed the working light bulb from the kitchen and was about to climb up on the cushioned chair in the breakfast room to complete the transfer when she heard: "Sandra! Sandra!" It was Lady Lucan calling from the top of the stairs.

The next 'mystery' I am going to try to solve does not even appear in the list above. Why was Lord Lucan walking passed the house at that time that night?

It was a well-known fact that Lord Lucan frequently walked passed No. 46 of an evening "to check on his children". Just about all of his family and friends were aware of this habit. The question is: Just how much 'checking' of his children, in bed upstairs, would Lord Lucan have been able to carry out from the pavement below, or driving passed, at nine o'clock at night? Not much, I fear!

Lord Lucan had lost custody of his children. He may have lost the battle, but he was still engaged in the war. Lucan continued his own surveillance. He employed detectives to watch the house and record the movements of both the Mother and her children, when the children were taken out, by whom, for how long, etc. Lucan is reported to have been seen parked outside No. 46, and he is known to have recorded conversations with his children. He had a pocket tape recorder, which he switched on when the conversations were headed in the 'right' direction.

If Lucan wanted to check on the well-being of his children, would it not make a lot of sense if he knocked on the basement door and spoke to the Nanny? And is that not precisely what Susan Maxwell-Scott told the Inquest that he did? (Ruddick p. 110):

> He started by saying that this [seeing the attack] was "an unbelievable co-incidence". I told him I didn't think so because he was in the habit of going past the house to check on the children. He said: "Well, yes. I quite often go in to see if the children are all right."

And there you have it: "go in". And the time that he is most likely to have done this is 9 p.m. His wife, having made her evening cup of tea, would have retired upstairs to watch the News on television before settling down for the night and would not be coming back downstairs again until the morning. The Court had ordered him to employ a Nanny. He paid her wages. Legally, the Nanny was answerable to him. Furthermore, he was the children's father. No one has ever questioned Lord Lucan's genuine love and affection for his three children or suggested that his concerns regarding the mental health of his wife were not sincere. The Nannies would probably have been in the basement at that time. Having put the children to bed, they would almost certainly have come downstairs to make themselves some supper, dinner with the children having been taken quite early. The Nannies would, of course, have invited him in. If the Nanny was having her evening cup of tea, and if the conversation took some time, it is possible that they may even have taken a cup of tea together, which is what I suspect may have been happening as he and the latest Nanny gradually became more friendly.

When preparing her book, *A Different Class of Murder*, published in 2014, Laura Thompson interviewed not only Veronica's sister, Jane, but also Sandra's sister, Teresa, and some of the Nannies, whom she managed to track down. The Nannies spoke of conversations they had with Lord Lucan about the children, not particularly specifying when or where these talks took place, but they support the suggestion that Lucan called in at No. 46 quite frequently.

Was that all he was planning that night? Possibly. At this point, I must confess that I fear he had more in mind.

Was an incipient affair sufficient reason for Lucan to kill his wife? If so, he would certainly have made sure that his new love was not on the premises. He would have known about the alteration to Sandra's time off. No. That would make no sense at all.

Back to the list of questions: Why had Lord Lucan been so anxious to borrow the Ford Corsair?

During a meal at the Portland Club, on Wednesday, 23rd October, Lucan had asked his good friend, Michael Stoop, if he could borrow Stoop's old Ford Corsair. Stoop offered him the use of his Mercedes, which Lucan declined. Stoop assumed that Lucan was declining the better car out of manners, but the important point to be noted here is that Lucan wanted the use of the car that night. "So Stoop told Lucan to get it insured and said that he would leave the car keys in the car outside his garage ... He [Lucan] then told Stoop to keep the matter secret" (Ruddick p. 66). Clearly Lucan needed a car which would not be recognized as his, one, indeed, which would not be noticed. He had an 'appointment' to keep!

We have no way of knowing whether that appointment was with Sandra or some other person. Lord and Lady Lucan had been separated for twenty-two months. Lucan was about to turn forty. No doubt he was ready for another relationship, and Nanny Rivett was just the type of woman he liked! Petite! 5 ft. 2 ins. tall - exactly the same height as his wife! There is no direct evidence that the two were starting a 'relationship' but I do think there is some circumstantial evidence.

Now, 23rd October, 1974, the evening on which Lucan first borrowed the Corsair, was a Wednesday. It was not Sandra Rivett's evening off. Either he was not meeting Sandra, or he was meeting with her at No. 46. There has never been any suggestion that Lord Lucan had any extra-marital affair during the time he was living with Lady Lucan. Nor is there any evidence, or even suggestion, that he had had any form of dalliance with any other woman during the twenty-two months of their separation. Lord Lucan was not a philanderer. He wanted a car that would not be recognized - parked outside No. 46. He knew Stoop had one that he never used. He asked Stoop not to tell anyone that he had borrowed it. Whatever it was that he was planning, he wanted the matter kept secret. I think all the available evidence points to Lord Lucan being just about to embark on an affair or some other surreptitious behaviour. It may not have been with Sandra, but it equally well may have been.

We have a small clue. Reference has already been made to the fact that Lucan recorded his children's conversations in the car. He had done so the previous weekend during the long drive to his sister's house in Northamptonshire. About sixty tapes were found, including that one. We know that he asked his youngest daughter, Camilla, about Nanny. When was her evening off? Did she have any boyfriends? Camilla told him that Sandra had mentioned two. One drove a Mercedes and lived in Lower Belgrave Street! It does not really matter whether this gentleman was Lord Lucan, or some other Mercedes owning resident of Lower Belgrave Street. What matters is that Camilla was aware of his existence. Sandra was clearly raising her sights when it came to 'boy friends'! This conversation has been taken as evidence of Lucan determining Sandra's evening off. As her employer, if he did not already know, he could have asked. No! When a man asks about an attractive lady's possible boyfriends, that is because he is interested! Slim evidence, maybe, but valid, I feel.

In Part I, outlining Sandra's biography, I mentioned the evidence that Sandra was a 'sex worker' of some description. I told of the empty flat in Kenley that she kept on after she went to work in London, of the picture of the nude male above her bed. Also discussed was Lucan's tendency towards S and M, as related by Lady Lucan. It would certainly seem that the two were well suited. And so the scene was set.

Life was good for Sandra. She was earning well above the usual wage as well as receiving free food and accommodation. Her duties were light. All three of her charges, even little Camilla, attended school. There were no night feeds or nappy changes. While her parents and her child were living in a caravan, she was living in a beautifully decorated house in one of the more expensive areas of London. She had a spare flat which she appears to have used for a lucrative side-line. Perhaps we should add to the list of her similarities with Lady Lucan a tendency to narcissism?

If Lucan had been planning to take Sandra out somewhere, he would have had money with him. He did not. Mention has already been made of the fact that he did not even have enough money to buy postage stamps for the letters he posted from Uckfield and Newhaven. Sandra would not have left the house, even when Lady Lucan was home, during a time when she was 'on call' – nor would Lord Lucan have dreamt of leaving the children alone in the house with Lady Lucan, even if they were in bed asleep. If they had planned to meet, they had planned to meet at No. 46, and the place where they would have met would have been the basement breakfast room. Sandra was quite entitled to have friends over in the evening. Lady Lucan was asked during the Inquest whether she ever did and she replied 'not that she knew of'. However, if Lady Lucan was in her bedroom, watching television, with her door shut, how likely is it that she would have known if Sandra had a visitor?

I wondered why Lucan even needed a car, since Elizabeth Street, where he was living, was only a couple of hundred yards away. He could easily have walked. Maybe it was the English weather? Whatever had been the situation on Wednesday, 23rd October, we do know that the weather was wet and windy on the night of 7th November. This has been recorded as one of the possible factors which may have contributed to Lucan's disappearance - presumed death by drowning - a simple overturning of the boat in which he was trying to escape.

Lord Lucan had declined the offer of a ticket to see Cole Porter performing at Blackfriars, which had been made to him by Greville Howard, a good friend, who was currently the tenant of the Lucan's Mews property, just around the corner at 5 Eaton Row. Lucan did, however, invite the theatre party to join him for dinner at the Clermont, booking a table for 11 p.m. If he were trying to keep an affair secret, it would have been imperative for him to be seen to continue his other activities as usual. He would have needed to put in an appearance at the Clermont. Lucan phoned the dinner booking through to the office at 8.30 p.m. Approximately fifteen minutes later, 8.45 p.m., Lucan, in his Mercedes, pulled up outside the Clermont and spoke to the 'linkman', without getting out of his car, enquiring whether any of his friends had arrived. He was told that no one was there yet and Lucan drove away. It has been suggested that Lucan made this short stop at the Clermont to establish an alibi for the time at which he had planned for Lady Lucan to be killed by his accomplice. However, as with so many incidents, there is another explanation.

At about 4.45 p.m. that afternoon (before he received the offer of the ticket to the theatre), Lucan had contacted a friend, Michael Hicks-Beach, to ask him to come to Elizabeth Street that evening to read through an article which Lucan had written for a student magazine about gambling. (Do as I say, not as I do?). He wanted Hicks-Beach's professional opinion about the piece before he submitted it. He had suggested the time of 6.30 p.m. After their meeting, Lucan drove Hicks-Beach home to Chelsea at around 8 p.m. He would probably have been back at Elizabeth Street somewhere around 8.30 p.m. The early time could be seen as suggesting that Lucan had something else in mind for the time between dropping Hicks-Beach back home and keeping the dinner appointment at the Clermont at 11 p.m.

It would appear that Lucan changed cars before his short trip to the Clermont. A friend, Andrina, had passed the Elizabeth Street place that afternoon and stated that the Mercedes was not there, so presumably Lucan was driving it that afternoon. Hicks-Beach, however, said that Lucan drove him home in a different car. Then he seems to have changed back to the Mercedes for the brief trip to the Clermont before changing once more to the Corsair for the evening. Interestingly, Ruddick (p. 77) reported that, when the Police found the Mercedes later that night, it had a flat battery. Batteries, in those days, did not die suddenly. One had warning that they were coming to the end of their life - pull out the choke, pump the accelerator and keep turning the ignition, it was worth several minutes of trying before giving up. If the battery did respond, a half-hour drive was recommended to recharge it. It would seem that the Mercedes' battery was dying. Lucan got it going that afternoon, but decided not to risk it for the drive to Chelsea - he could hardly expect his passenger to sit in the passenger seat while he kept pumping the engine! When he returned, about 8.30 p.m., he tried the Mercedes again and it started. He took it for a short drive, as far as the Clermont and back, but he did not turn the engine off - the purpose of the short drive was to recharge the battery, hence his talking to the linkman from the car. He then drove home and swapped to the Corsair for the evening. Ruddick (p. 116) mentioned that there was a battery charger, which Stoop confirmed belonged to him, inside the Corsair when it was found. Had Lucan used it to start the Mercedes that one last time? Probably!

That short stop made by Lucan outside the Clermont was pivotal to the investigation. If Sandra was attacked before 9 p.m., her attacker could not be Lord Lucan. As part of his investigations, Marnham drove several times from the Clermont Club to Lucan's residence in Elizabeth Street, which is where the Mercedes was later found parked. The shortest time taken was 7 minutes. In fact, if the times given by Lady Frances (which differed from those given by Lady Lucan) were correct, then Lucan did, indeed, have an alibi for the attack on Sandra Rivett, if that attack took place before 9 p.m. Lady Frances gave 9.05 p.m. as the time Lucan ushered Lady Lucan back into her bedroom. Just before 9 p.m. is the earliest possible time for Lucan to have arrived at No. 46. This fact is universally accepted. If Lucan killed Sandra before attacking Lady Lucan, then he could not possibly have been in the bedroom at 9.05 p.m. Lady Lucan gave the time as 9.25 p.m., which made her arrival at the Plumbers Arms at 9.45 p.m. a little more plausible.

There were several discrepancies between the times given by Lady Lucan and Lady Frances. Lady Lucan gave 8.55 p.m. as the time Sandra popped her head around the door, offering to make the tea. This, of course, was the time at which Lady Lucan would normally have made the tea for herself, so does make some sense. However, there is something compelling about Lady Frances' account (Ruddick pp.19-20):

> I stayed in the Nursery and then went downstairs to Mummy's bedroom. That would have been about 8.40 p.m.
>
> I asked Mummy where Sandra was and Mummy said she was downstairs making some tea. After a while, Mummy said she wondered why Sandra was taking so long. I don't know what time it was but it was before the news came on the television at 9 p.m.

Lady Frances gave the time that her parents entered the bedroom together as 9.05 p.m. She also stated that (Marnham p. 183):

> "Mummy, Camilla, George and Sandra were downstairs watching The Six Million Dollar Man. I joined them at 8.05 and we all watched TV in Mummy's room. When the programme finished at 8.30 I went back to the Nursery …".

This implies that Sandra was in Lady Lucan's bedroom from shortly after 8 p.m. until 8.30 p.m. It was Sandra's parents who gave evidence that Sandra had telephoned them shortly after 8 p.m. It must be remembered that long distance calls were far more expensive then than they are now. During the 1960s, 'STD' (Subscriber Trunk Dialling) was being introduced. Previously all long-distance (Trunk) calls had been connected through an operator and were charged in three-minute increments. After three minutes, the operator would ask if the caller wanted to extend. More and more areas became STD, but the price stayed the same. People were very aware of the cost of Trunk calls and it is possible that Sandra's call home at (approximately) 8 p.m. was short, completed by (approximately) 8.05 p.m. To the evidence of the telephone call must be added 'evidence' that Sandra spent some time in her bedroom, ironing. Lady Lucan later said that Sandra had done some ironing in her room at around 8.30 p.m. This would be consistent with Sandra having ironed after putting the two younger children to bed and before coming down and making the offer of tea just before, or even just after, 9 p.m., which was Lady Lucan's timeline. It is inconsistent with Sandra having offered to make Lady Lucan's tea shortly after 8.30 p.m., and with Sandra already being making the tea when Lady Frances went back into the bedroom at 8.40 p.m. I believe Lady Frances because she had no reason to lie, whereas Lady Lucan had every reason to delay the time line as much as she could. We only have Lady Lucan's word that Sandra did any ironing at all.

When Lady Frances was not sure about time, she said so. Lady Lucan made a clear error in relation to time, saying that she arrived at the Plumbers' Arms at 9.55 p.m., whereas the people present at the Pub evidenced the time at which she arrived as having been 9.45 p.m. Lady Lucan's mistake is all the more surprising since it extended the time she spent with Lord Lucan after the attack. Her statement made it sound as though, having lain on the bed, with the towel on the pillow, and Lord Lucan having gone into the *en suite*, she made an immediate escape. There was a clear advantage to her giving later times for the attack. It allowed time for Lucan to have been the perpetrator after his brief visit to the Clermont. It is unlikely that Lady Lucan learnt of the Clermont visit until she was recovering, which would help account for her changing, extending, the time in her later accounts. She gave the time of their return to the bedroom as 9.25 p.m. Not arriving at the *Plumbers Arms* until 9.45 p.m. meant that she had not run out of the house until about 9.43 p.m., eighteen minutes later. Why she added a further ten minutes is difficult to understand, yet she had plenty of time to go over the times in her mind since her statement was not taken by the Police until 6 p.m. Friday evening.

I have accepted Lady Frances' time line. She had no reason to lie. Veronica did. I further believe that, when Sandra made her offer in relation to the making of tea at approximately 8.35 p.m., Lady Lucan presumed that she had already put Lady Frances to bed. She would have been surprised when Lady Frances came into the room. It would not have taken long for her sharp mind to have realized that something was going on. She said she was going to check on the tea. I think she was going to check on Sandra!

Now we must return to Sandra. What do we know about what she was doing during this time?

Ruddick (p. 69) wrote: "Sandra had rung her parents in Basingstoke to tell them how much she was looking forward to coming home for Christmas, and had then gone to her room to finish some ironing". Unless Sandra had her own phone in her bedroom, the phone call would have been made from the basement. There would have been a phone there for the use of the staff when placing household orders, etc. Ruddick said that she had then "gone to her room to finish some ironing". Assuming that Sandra did, indeed, do some ironing, what ironing was she doing? Why did Sandra not do her ironing while in the basement? One answer might be that it was too dark - the light bulb had blown - but we know that the bulb on the chair was functioning because it worked when replaced in the socket by Sergeant Baker when he first entered the basement.

Was the family ironing so urgent that it could not wait until morning? Sandra had little enough to do during the day, while the children were at school. I cannot think that she would have needed to carry the family's ironing upstairs to her bedroom on the third/fourth floor after 8 p.m. at night. It seems more likely that Sandra would have been doing 'personal' ironing in her room at that time of night.

There is nothing untoward in Sandra ironing her own clothes in her own room. It is only the time which is strange. According to Lady Frances, Sandra was watching TV with the family at that time. It does not really matter whether Sandra ironed after 8 p.m., or earlier, perhaps while one of the older children was bathing? What is interesting is that she should have felt the need to do any personal ironing when it was not her evening off. She was not going out. A quick press of an item about to be worn, to freshen it up after hanging in the cupboard for a few days, that is quite standard female practice. I feel that this is a further indication that Sandra may have been expecting a visitor that night, although I have my doubts about the whole ironing episode.

Unfortunately, we do not know Sandra's usual evening routine. All we know is what it was not. Sandra did not usually make Lady Lucan's evening cup of tea. Lady Lucan usually came down to the basement to make that for herself. I have already stated my conclusion that the children were all put to bed by 8.30 p.m., which was Sandra's 'knocking off' time. She would not have been on duty at 9 p.m. Lady Lucan would have had to make her own tea at that time. Sandra may usually have left the basement by then, having made her own snack and taken it up to her room. Equally, she may usually have eaten her snack in the basement and still been there when Lady Lucan came down to make her own tea. Whatever was her usual routine, Sandra changed it that night.

It seems to me logical to assume that Sandra would normally have taken Lady Frances up to bed before going down to the basement apartment to make herself a cup of tea and possibly some supper, tea with the children having been at 5.30 p.m. With no more official duties until 7 a.m., unless one of the children woke in the night, what would normally have happened then? Would Sandra also have changed into more casual clothes? Possibly. Did she rejoin Lady Lucan, watching T.V. in the bedroom? No, probably not. Had she done that, then I think almost certainly she would have made the tea at 9 p.m. Even though the two women were living under the same roof, they probably had strict, if unwritten, rules about personal space. When the work day was done, both Lady Lucan and Sandra would enjoy their brief independence. Sandra was the Nanny, not the housekeeper. She was not responsible for the preparation of Lady Lucan's food or drink. If Lady Lucan wanted a cup of tea after Sandra's 'knocking off' time, the making of it would definitely have been her responsibility.

What would seem to be obvious is that, when Lady Lucan made her tea, she would have come down to the kitchen at a time when Sandra could also have been there. If the upstairs front room was indeed the Nursery, then whichever of the bedrooms was Sandra's, it was only small. She may have stayed in the basement for a while, or she may have gone back up to the Nursery to watch television. Whatever was her usual routine, I doubt that she changed into casual clothes. This night she did. She was expecting a visitor a visitor - a visitor Sandra did not wish Lady Lucan to meet! I have concluded that Sandra's unusual offer with regard to the tea was made with the intention of insuring that Lady Lucan did not go down to the kitchen that night. There had to be a reason and I cannot think of another one.

We are now coming to the crucial part of the evening. This is the time when we have been led to believe that someone, either Lord Lucan or his accomplice, entered No. 46, found Sandra in the basement, bludgeoned her, killed her, and then attacked Lady Lucan. The killing of Sandra Rivett was a mistake. The plan had been to kill Lady Lucan.

We are also led to believe that this murder had been some time (at least two weeks) in the planning.

Defenders of Lord Lucan have suggested that Lord Lucan, even if he had wished his wife were dead, even if he had planned to kill her, or have her killed, would never run the risk of his children seeing their Mother's dead body. This being the case, the 'intruder' scenario, a 'burglary gone wrong', which would have necessitated Veronica's body being found in the kitchen, would have been discounted. They argued that, in the unlikely event of his having planned Lady Lucan's death, Lucan would have insisted upon a scenario which suggested that, in a fit of depression, Veronica had walked out - and disappeared.

Why was not a pillow put over Lady Lucan's face while she lay sleeping? Why did Lord Lucan not call round one evening with a silk scarf in his pocket? A man of Lucan's build would have had no difficulty in carrying Veronica's dead body out to the car. If he could not face doing the job himself, his accomplice could, surely, easily have carried the body out?

There were no security cameras in those days and, even if someone had seen a bundle being put into the boot of a car, and even if they did remember the make and model of the car, the chances of such a car being traced, would have been small. So long as Lucan was at the Clermont at the time, he would have been in the clear. To Lucan's supporters, the concept of Lucan having set out to kill Veronica himself was unthinkable, and that of Lucan deliberately putting himself at the scene of the crime, unthinkably stupid. The idea that Lucan borrowed the Corsair because the boot in the Mercedes was too small was unthinkably ludicrous.

To assume that Lucan, despite all the surveillance he was undertaking, both on his own and with a hired detective agency, was unaware of the change that week to Sandra's day off, does seem rather extraordinary. Even more extraordinary, apparently, neither Lucan, nor his accomplice, thought to watch the house ahead of the planned crime to make sure Sandra had, indeed, left the premises before the accomplice entered!

Next to be considered would have been what weapon should be used? Now, I think killers usually provide their own weapons but, even if Lord Lucan had offered to be the supplier, I cannot believe that any self-respecting professional (or even amateur) killer, would accept the proffered small piece of lead piping. If Lord Lucan (or his paid accomplice) were planning to murder Lady Lucan, do you not think they would have armed themselves with something more substantial than this piece of malleable lead? A tyre iron from the boot of the car perhaps? Or a child's cricket bat? Lord Lucan was 6' 4" tall. The width of his hand would have been around 5". A 5" hand grasped around a 9" piece of piping does not leave much for striking.

Consider the choice of material – lead. Lead is heavy, it is non corrosive and it is malleable. These three characteristics made lead the number one material of choice for pipes for centuries. Indeed, the very word 'plumber' comes from the Latin word for lead: plumbum. After its toxic effects were recognized, it was replaced by copper or plastic. A long piece might be difficult to hide walking down the street, although it has not been suggested that Lucan walked. This might have led to the consideration of a shorter length – if the material had been iron or steel. Not lead. In years not so very much gone by, it was possible to buy small strips of lead at the local Pet Shop, to wind around the roots of small aquatic plants before dropping them into an aquarium, to make sure the plants remained on the bottom until they rooted. The lead was so soft that the strip could easily be wound a couple of times round the delicate plants. These strips are no longer available, lead being poisonous. Whether their banning was to protect the health of the humans or the fish I am not sure!

This was a short (9") piece of lead piping – not a solid

rod or a bar, but a hollow piece of piping. We are told its length and its weight, 2½ lbs., but not its diameter, but if the re-enactment in the Documentary of Lord Lucan strapping a small length of wood with which he 'beat' Lady Lucan is to be taken as any guide, it was quite moderate in thickness. Since Lady Lucan herself was the major participant in the Documentary, I cannot believe that the Director would not have taken guidance from Lady Lucan on this point. Be that as it may, we are never told the diameter of the piping used that night, but it clearly was not very sturdy, since it had so easily bent out of shape. It was mistaken, at first, for the leg of a doll.

Of the fact that this was the implement used to hit both Lady Lucan and Sandra Rivett there has never been any question. What I do believe should be questioned is the purpose for which this implement had been constructed. Not to commit murder, of that I am certain.

I think the clue is to be found in what Sandra Rivett was wearing when her body was found in the bag. Black tights.

When Sergeant Baker lifted the flap of the bloody canvass bag in the kitchen that night, he saw "part of a human thigh in black tights" (Ruddick p. 10). Tights! Not jeans, or trousers, or a skirt, or a dress, but tights. According to Thompson (p. 223), Sandra was wearing "a flowered smock over her dress". The flowered smock sounds right. Loose tops over tights or close-fitting jeans were very popular and would have been very acceptable casual wear. The 'dress' is more problematic. Sandra had been bent over; her head and feet had been placed in the bag first, which is why her buttocks were near the opening. If she was wearing a skirt, and the skirt had ridden up, which is, of course, quite possible, then the skirt would have bunched up around her thighs and should have been the first piece of clothing visible. That her hand was seen at the same time as her buttock shows that her hands were down beside her body, in the normal anatomical position. Had Sandra been wearing a dress, as suggested, and had it ridden up, then her arms/hands would also have prevented the dress riding up past her buttocks. Her clothing does seem to have been 'casual'. The question is, when did she change? Had she already changed before she put her head round Lady Lucan's bedroom door? Is that why she did not go in? And why was she making the tea before putting Lady Frances to bed? If she was still on duty, as she would have been until Lady Frances was in bed, then her clothing was inappropriate. And then there is that perennial question: Why the offer of tea? And why then, nearly half-an-hour before Lady Lucan's usual time?

Sandra's shoes were by the sack. They were a simple pair of black court shoes, quite appropriate for wearing with the smock and tights, off duty. But Lady Frances was not yet in bed. Sandra Rivett was still on duty. It keeps coming back to those three things: the tea, Sandra's clothes and why Lady Frances was not put to bed at the usual time. I think the delay is an integral part of the whole unfolding saga. Lady Frances was expecting Sandra to collect her from the Nursery. She was sufficiently puzzled by the delay to go downstairs to her Mother's room to try to find out what was happening. The usual routine had been broken. Lady Frances was not the only person to be puzzled. So was Veronica and she went downstairs to find the answer.

The couple (John and Sandra) only had a short amount of time for their assignation. Even if Lucan had not made the dinner appointment with the theatre party, he would still have needed to be seen at the Clermont at the usual time. John would have needed to return to Elizabeth Street, bath/shower and dress before leaving for the Clermont. As the host, he would have been expected to be first at the table, to welcome his guests. He would have needed to leave No. 46 by 10.30 p.m. at the latest. Even arriving promptly at 9 p.m. did not give the couple a great deal of time and I suspect Sandra did expect John to arrive promptly! Nine o'clock was just after Lady Lucan usually made her tea. I suspect Sandra wanted to ensure that Lady Lucan was well out of the way so she conceived the plan of taking Lady Lucan her tea early.

After putting the two younger children to bed, Sandra quickly changed into more comfortable clothing, which she should not have done quite so early, which is why she only popped her head around the door. Lady Lucan did not see what she was wearing. Confident that Lady Frances would play happily in the Nursery for a while longer, Sandra set about her tea making. Then, I suspect, it was her plan to take the tray upstairs and say to Lady Frances: "I have made your Mother's tea. Why don't you take it in to her?" Children (especially girls!) love these role reversals and I am sure, that had that happened, Lady Frances would have taken the tray from Sandra, with scarcely a thought as to what she was wearing at that time of night, and have proudly delivered the expected tea, with a broad smile across her face! Sandra would have put her smiling face around the door again, not showing her casual clothes, and then sent Lady Frances up to bed.

Quite why Sandra was so keen to be ready for her assignation so early, we will never know but she may well have wanted to prepare something special for John. It may have been as simple as a special 'something' with the evening cup of tea. That's the sort of thing people do at the beginning of a relationship. Whatever it was, she needed to prepare it before 9 p.m., before Lady Lucan came down to make her last cup of tea.

Now we come to the most important part. In the Documentary, Lady Lucan, without any apparent leading by the interviewer, told how her husband had one day said he would 'beat the mad ideas' out of her. She was 'made' to kneel on the floor, with her hands on the seat of a chair, while he delivered ten strokes to her buttocks with a piece of stick, which had had bound with tape. She went on to explain that the strokes were measured, "he could have hit harder". He repeated this behaviour on two other occasions. Each time, she said, he would be very affectionate afterwards and look regretfully at the damage he had caused.

Not surprisingly, the interviewer had asked if Lord Lucan had sado-masochistic tendencies, whether he took pleasure from the 'beatings' he gave her. After a short pause, Lady Lucan had replied: "He must have got pleasure from them because we had intercourse afterwards". Then she had done something rather extraordinary. She had leant forward toward the interviewer and said:

> "But he obviously must have thought about it because when I opened my cupboard, there was a stick hanging there, with the end cut off and wrapped in plasters so that it would not hurt so much. So he had to have been thinking about doing it and the truncheon was covered in plaster, bandaged exactly the same as the stick hanging up in the cupboard. I just think that's very strange."

The interviewer then asked her if she had just made the connection - just now? - to which Lady Lucan replied:

> Yes. So I just mentioned to you what he did. That's the connection. He wanted to do it. And then ... Why did he wrap plaster on the bludgeon? Why? I just don't know.

Now, the police already knew that the piping had belonged to Lord Lucan, thanks to the similar piece found in the back of the Ford Corsair. Indeed, it was the primary piece of evidence leading to an assumption of Lord Lucan's guilt. Lady Lucan did not need to mention the S & M to establish that fact. As far as I know, the S & M behaviour was not known to investigators, either the Police or authors, until the Documentary, which was not released until June, 2017. Why did Lady Lucan bring the subject up? What was she trying to tell the Interviewer, or, for that matter, the viewer? She must have been trying to make the interviewer understand the purpose for which the piping implement (truncheon) had been constructed. If it was not for use on her that night, then upon whom was Lord Lucan planning to use it? It must have been Sandra, but not in the way that the police and other experts had put forward at the Inquest. By introducing, without any prompting, the subject of sado-masochism, of stressing the similarity of the 'weapon' used on her with that of the weapon she claimed Lord Lucan had bought with him that night, what was she trying to say? That Lord Lucan was intending to indulge in a fourth S & M session with her but hit her on the head instead of the buttocks? Hardly! If he was not intending to indulge in S & M with Veronica, then there is only one other person he can possibly have had in mind – Sandra!

I am sure I do not need to remind you of Sandra's extra flat in Kenley, with that picture of the nude male hanging over the bed! Surely, one is entitled to make a deduction?

People do not develop sado-masochistic tendencies for no reason. That some people might enjoy the sense of power, of being the deliverer of punishment rather than the receiver, may be relatively easy to understand. It is well known that abused children often grow up to become abusive parents. Acting out the role reversal in a controlled manner is definitely to be preferred. Why, some may wonder, would anyone voluntarily subject themselves to being the receiver – the masochist? The explanation generally offered is that young children often experience pleasure after experiencing pain. The infant, or toddler, is smacked, or punished in some way, for some misdemeanour, possibly, even probably, without being truly aware of the transgression for which he/she is being punished, and then comforted afterwards. Take, for example, the scenario of a baby pulling itself into the upright position by clutching the tablecloth. Its mother sees the items on the table start to move towards her aspiring toddler. There may even be hot food on the table. She screams, grabs the child, smacks his/her hand to make him/her release grip on the cloth. The bewildered child howls. And then what? The mother holds her precious child close to her chest. She rocks him/her, talks soothingly, may even give the child a sweet or a biscuit. Such scenarios are part of any child's experience but, for some children, they occur more frequently than others, especially if one, or both, parents are habitually temperamental or abuse alcohol. So it is that some people enjoy the victim role and the 'making up' afterwards.

As Lord Lucan came to know the new Nanny, one can imagine that, during the course of conversations about the children, Lucan and Sandra chatted about life in London and what Sandra did on her night off.? Perhaps she mentioned visiting certain night clubs and the conversation led from one thing to another, as conversations tend to do. It has been suggested that Lucan had first made the larger of the two implements, then, realizing that the ceiling was not as high in the basement as in the rooms upstairs, had made the second, shorter version. Presumably, it was supposed, he brought the larger weapon as a back-up. No other explanation is offered for its presence in the boot of the car.

As always, there is another possible explanation.

Assuming John's preference was for the 'sadist' role, had he made the 9" rod for use during a previous meeting? Had he left it with Sandra? (He must have done, because it was used before he arrived.) Had he made it small, because Sandra was small? Was the longer piece in the boot intended for an 'enhancement' of their activities? Did they swap roles? Were the two pieces 'His' and 'Hers'? I feel this is just as likely as Lucan having made a second, shorter piece, in case he (or his accomplice) accidentally hit the ceiling.

If Lord Lucan arrived, saw the basement was in darkness, left the car, went down the basement steps to look through the window to check whether Sandra was in or not, then his leaving his S & M implement in the boot of the car while he was checking makes good sense. Sandra already had the smaller implement with her. She must have done.

There are only four people in whose possession it could possibly have been: Lord Lucan, the accomplice, Lady Lucan or Sandra. There are only two possibilities: either the weapon was already in the house or the attacker brought it with him. The first possibility never seems to have been entertained. It should have been.

The Police always accepted the testimony of the linkman at the Clermont, that Lord Lucan was in his car, outside, at 8.45 p.m., or thereabouts. They accepted that it would not have been possible for Lord Lucan to have driven home, changed cars, made his way to the house and attacked Sandra Rivett before 9 p.m. Using Lady Lucan's later time frame, her not checking on Sandra until after the News had started, made Lord Lucan a possible suspect in the eyes of some people, although the timing was tight. Enter 'the accomplice'. The Police claimed that the weapon was in the possession of the accomplice, even though there had never been any evidence for the presence of any other person in the house that night. Nevertheless, the accomplice was still considered to be a possibility, but only if it was allowed that the accomplice had agreed to use a weapon supplied by Lucan. Lady Lucan definitely did not have it. That leaves Sandra – for me, the most likely candidate.

We have now come to the point at which Lady Lucan was at the top of the basement stairs, calling down to Sandra. Sandra was somewhere in the basement apartment, wearing whatever it was that she was wearing and doing whatever it was that she was doing – making tea? changing the light bulb? The question is: Where was the weapon? Where was the implement at the moment Lady Lucan called down the basement stairs to Sandra?

If Sandra was, indeed, in the process of changing the light bulb, it is unlikely that she was holding the piping in her hand. Had she tucked it into her waistband? Or, on her way down, had she placed it on the small hall table near the basement stairs? One way or another, that weapon made it to the top of the basement stairs, because that is where Lady Lucan was attacked with it. Lady Frances testified that "Just after she [Lady Lucan] left the room, I heard a scream. It sounded as though it came from a long way away". Lady Frances assumed that the scream came from her Mother, possibly scratched by the cat, but, receiving no response to her call, she retreated into the bedroom and shut the door. 'A long way away" does not sound like the bottom of the main stairs, in the hall, but more like somewhere on the basement stairs – not necessarily at the top, and the scream may have come from either Lady Lucan or Sandra.

Sandra, hearing Lady Lucan call, left the breakfast room and went up the stairs. Etiquette demanded that she must ascend the stairs rather than Lady Lucan descend them. Neurotic/paranoid Lady Lucan may have been, but stupid she was not! If the implement was tucked into Sandra's waistband, or on the hall table, she would have known what she was seeing!

At the Inquest, the medical examiner was quite specific. Sandra Rivet had not been attacked from behind as the Police had at first supposed. The first blow had been struck from the front. It consisted of a hard slap across one cheek, followed by a lighter punch to the other. I propose that Lady Lucan struck Sandra Rivett a strong blow across her face with an open hand and then struck her for a second time with a 'back-hander'. Sandra responded by grabbing Lady Lucan by the hair. I had been puzzled by the amount of Lady Lucan's hair which had been found on the 'murder' weapon, stuck to blood on the wall and in 'bunches' on the towel which had been placed over the pillow in the bedroom. Why was so much of Lady Lucan's hair found at the scene, but none of Sandra's? This was never explained, or even commented on that I could see. Had Lady Lucan recently been sick, suffered a high temperature? No! The two protagonists became embroiled in a 'cat fight'!

At the Inquest, the pathologist noted that Lady Lucan's neck had been 'wrenched', although there were no marks on it. It was, of course, assumed that this injury had been inflicted by Lord Lucan, but, to me, the lack of 'marks' (i.e. bruising) is more consistent with Sandra having grabbed Lady Lucan by the hair and yanked it. At some point Sandra grabbed the 'stick' and struck Lady Lucan six times across the forehead. One can imagine it - whack, whack, whack, whack, whack, whack - back and forth three times. The lacerations made a 'V' shape in the top centre of Lady Lucan's forehead and were so 'neat' in appearance that the surgeon had difficulty telling where one wound ended and another commenced. Sixty stitches were required, approximately ten per wound, if that helps you visualize the length of wounds.

How long the struggle lasted, who can tell, but probably not for more than a couple of minutes. Lady Lucan began to bleed freely. Sandra probably realized that enough was enough. She turned and ran down the stairs, one hand holding the balustrade. In the darkness, she tripped over the tray, which she had placed on one of the lower steps. (If she was wearing her high heels, no wonder she tripped!). As she fell, she flung out the other hand, hitting the picture hanging on the wall at the bottom of the basement stairs, which was found askew. The hand grasping the balustrade pulled her sideways. As she fell she hit her head/face on the end of the balustrade (Newell post), causing her nose to bleed which resulted in the two pools of blood, one at the base of the stairs and the other where she fell. As she lost consciousness, she staggered forward/sideways about 4 ft. (probably a distance approximate to the height of your armpit) before falling near the piano, choking on her own blood as the result of the nose bleed.

Lady Lucan picked up the weapon which had fallen by her side and, in a fury, rained down a series of blows. The medical examiner stated quite clearly that the blows which Sandra received had been struck after she lost consciousness. He deduced this from the fact that the blows were 'in parallel'. Sandra had not moved her head at all, had not tried to avoid any other blows, some of which missed her head, striking her on the neck, shoulders or upper back.

Exhausted and hysterical, Lady Lucan, who had no idea

of the extent of the damage which Sandra had suffered, ran back up the stairs, at the top of which she encountered Lord Lucan. He, by the 'incredible co-incidence' which he told both his mother and Susan Maxwell-Scott had happened, had peered through the kitchen window just in time to witness the end of the assault. How much he saw, we will never know. Veronica hitting Sandra? Veronica running back up the stairs? John immediately ran back up the outside basement stairs, let himself in through the front door, ran down the hallway, where he found Lady Lucan, battered and bleeding. From his position outside, he may not have realized that she had been attacked and was bleeding freely. It may well have been Lady Lucan, not Lord Lucan, who was in the washroom. After all, it was her blood which was found there.

The Police rejected the claim that Lucan had seen an assult taking place. An officer standing on the pavement reported that it was not possible to see, from there, into the basement. The open venetian blinds obscured any vision from that angle. When kneeling down, he could see a little way onto the bench, but that was all. The Police never considered that Lucan may have descended the steps to look through the window. I am sure that is what he would have done if the basement was unexpectedly in darkness.

Lady Lucan claimed that she was hysterical. I don't think anyone has ever questioned that part of her evidence. Lady Lucan also claimed that her hysterical state was caused by Lord Lucan trying to push her down the stairs and her desperate struggle to stop him. Lucan had thrust three gloved fingers down her throat, which she claimed he did in an attempt to throttle her. I have never heard of anyone trying to throttle another person by putting three fingers, gloved or otherwise, down their throat. Around the throat, yes! Down it, no! What I have heard of, and, indeed, seen, is someone putting their fingers down another person's throat to remove an obstruction, to prevent that person from choking. It is far more likely that Veronica, in her hysterical state, was half choking and that Lucan was checking her airway, rather than that he was trying to throttle her. Scratch marks on the back of Veronica's throat confirm that Lucan did do something.

Lady Lucan further claimed that, after a desperate struggle, she caused Lord Lucan to release her by grabbing hold of his genitals. After that, he quietened down and, following a short talk, they went upstairs together. Now, Gentlemen, I have a question for you. If you were fighting with someone - your wife, for example - whom you were trying to kill, and that person grabbed you by the genitals, would that calm you down, or make you more angry? Yes. That's what I thought. Nevertheless, the Police accepted Lady Lucan's explanation of how she quietened her husband, first by grasping his genitals and then by 'talking him down' before they went upstairs together.

Now we are coming to a very important, and very interesting, part of the story. But first we must ask: What was Lord Lucan wearing that night?

Hicks-Beach told the Police that Lucan had been casually dressed when they met earlier that evening, that he was wearing flannels and a sweater (Thompson p. 214). Unfortunately, the colour of the sweater was not mentioned. We know that when he first arrived at No. 46, he was wearing gloves. What else was he wearing, besides gloves? According to Lady Frances, when he came up to the bedroom, after the murder, he was wearing "dark trousers and an overcoat, which was full length and was fawn coloured with dark check" (Thompson p. 242). Lady Lucan described his clothing as "a sweater of sorts, no tie and grey flannel trousers' (Thompson: p. 231). Considering it was November, an overcoat and gloves would make sense. Indeed, the casual clothing described by Lady Lucan made no sense at all as far as 'street' clothing was concerned. They made perfect sense as 'indoor' clothing in a well-heated house. According to Susan Maxwell-Scott, Lucan was not wearing the overcoat when he arrived at Uckfield. He was wearing grey trousers, blue shirt and a brown pullover, with no sleeves. A brown pullover with a blue shirt? There is no way those were the clothes Lucan was wearing when he left home! A grey-blue sweater, yes. Brown, no!

A number of greyish-blue wool fibres were found adhering to the binding on the piping. More were found in other parts of the house, in the downstairs cloakroom, on the towel in the bathroom and in the abandoned car. These fibres have never been identified, although it has been suggested that they were from Lucan's trousers, even though these were twice described as 'grey', not 'greyish-blue'. I believe Lucan was wearing a blue-grey woollen sweater when he arrived, which became soiled with blood when he tried to render assistance to Sandra before he realized that she was dead and later when he helped Veronica put the body in the mail bag. He changed into the brown pullover when they went back to the bedroom for the last time. He put the soiled sweater over the towel rail in the bathroom while he was washing, accounting for the fibres found there, picking it up again on leaving, before he realized that Veronica was missing. He still had it in his hand as he ran out of the door after Veronica. He threw it onto the passenger seat of the car, accounting for the blood evidence found in the car. He was still wearing the brown pullover when he arrived at the Maxwell-Scott's.

The item of clothing which deposited the blue-grey fibres has never been found. Nobody seems to have taken any notice of Lady Frances' observation and, therefore, nobody has bothered to question what happened to the overcoat. I believe Lady Frances, simply because of time of year; I do not believe anybody would go outdoors on an English November evening without a coat.

I am assuming that there were still a few bits and pieces belonging to Lucan at the house. When he left Veronica, he only took one bag with him. Lady Lucan insisted that she always thought that Lucan would come back. If he had only taken his belongings piecemeal, as he needed them, still leaving some bits and pieces at No. 46, that might have fuelled her misconception.

It was Lady Lucan's evidence that it was she who suggested that the pair of them should go upstairs to the bedroom. Why did she do this? One obvious reason is that she needed to lie down to recover from her exertions and her injuries. Could she have had any other thought in her mind? To reach the stairs, it was necessary for them to pass through the hall. Had she thought of trying to make a run for it at that point? If so, she was foiled by John, who, she recorded, had held her tightly. Lady Lucan was not alone in the house. Lady Frances was in the bedroom watching television. Was she hoping to enlist Lady Frances' help? She never did. Neither her own testimony, nor that of Lady Frances, intimates that Veronica made any effort whatsoever to alert Lady Frances to her predicament. On the contrary, it was she who told Lady Frances to go upstairs to bed. Then she lay down on the bed, placing herself in the most vulnerable position possible! She later explained her action to the Police as an attempt to lull Lord Lucan into a false sense of security. In that, she certainly succeeded. I have heard of victims co-operating with their assailants and the fact that they live to tell the tale bears witness to the fact that, on some occasions at least, the tactic works. The Police accepted that this was the case with Veronica.

In the Documentary, Lady Lucan claimed that Lucan had 'frogmarched' her upstairs to the bedroom. 'Frogmarching' is when one person holds another person's arm up behind their back, forcing them forward. This position would have prevented blood from Lady Lucan soiling Lord Lucan's clothes. Lady Sarah did not remember seeing any blood on her father's clothing. I think Lord Lucan took off his overcoat and hung it in the cupboard, probably putting his gloves on the shelf above. No further mention of the coat or gloves is made, although Lucan was wearing neither when he arrived at the Maxwell-Scott's. The subsequent examination of the crime scene seems to have been a complete shemozzle. I am not aware of any report of items found in the cupboards.

On arriving in the bedroom, and with Veronica resting on the towel on the bed, Veronica claimed in the Documentary and elsewhere that Lucan had asked her if she had any sleeping pills? She replied that she had and he took them from her. She then suggested that Lucan was planning to force her to swallow them and then, possibly, put a pillow over her face. Considering her history of previous suicide attempts, I think it is far more likely that John was removing temptation.

That 'talking-down'. What did Veronica say? By her account, Veronica told Lucan to leave. She would tell the Police that an intruder had attacked first Sandra, then her. No one need ever know that Lucan had been there. By her own account, she was always planning to escape at the first opportunity. She was always going to betray him. She expressed the need to lie down and took the opportunity to escape while Lucan was in the bathroom.

The problem with Lady Lucan's account is timing.

Originally, her account of when Sandra made her offer of tea was similar to that of Lady Frances. Then Lady Lucan made it closer to nine o'clock, even slightly after, which would have been quite ridiculous, since she would have made her own tea by then. If Lady Frances usually watched the evening News with Lady Lucan, as has been suggested, then she, too, would have seen Sandra puting her head round the door, making her unusual offer. The whole episode of Sandra putting her head around the door before Lady Frances came back into the room only makes sense accepting Lady Frances' timing.

Lady Lucan tried to delay everything. She gave 9.25 p.m. as the time she and Lucan came back upstairs and sent Lady Frances to bed. That still left nearly twenty minutes before she made her escape. Inexplicably, she then also extended the time of her arrival at the *Plumbers Arms* by ten minutes. Had she ever been cross examined, her whole story would have collapsed, but the peculiar rules surrounding evidence at the Inquest, which were in place at that time, prevented that.

After the struggle with his wife ended, and before frog-marching her upstairs, I feel sure that Lucan would have checked to see that Sandra was O.K., i.e. still alive and breathing. We know that by now her airways were already starting to become congested with blood. There may have been a slight rattle, in which case he would not even have needed to go down the stairs to check on her, hearing her breathing, but not realizing the significance of what he heard. Lucan would have been very surprised to see Lady Frances in the bedroom. She should have been in bed by now. Once she was dispatched, he would have inspected Lady Lucan's wounds, recommended that he take her to the hospital, which offer she would have refused, not trusting him not to take the opportunity to have her admitted to a psychiatric ward.

I believe that the two were together on that bed, he sitting, she lying on the towel because of the blood, he not needing one because, at that point of time there was no blood on his clothes. I believe both of them would have been listening for the sound of Sandra's footsteps as she came upstairs. They probably more than half expected Sandra to stop at the bedroom. The footsteps never came.

After a short time, it would have become clear to the pair of them that Lucan would have to go back down to the basement to check on Sandra, which he did. He found Sandra dead.

I think the first thing he would then have done would be return to the bedroom to tell his wife the terrible news. I believe that it was at this time that the "She's dead" conversation took place and I further believe that it was not Lady Lucan who has offering to help Lord Lucan, but the other way around! Of course, they should have contacted the Emergency Services, but they didn't. Instead, they decided to dispose of the body. People panic. They would not have been the first people to make a similar decision, nor the last. By then, it would have been somewhere between 9.15 p.m.–9.20 p.m.

After John had told Veronica what had happened, I believe both of them would have returned to the basement. They would have turned Sandra over, if John had not already done so. That would have been the time when Sandra's blood was transferred to Lucan's clothing – mostly to his blue-grey sweater, but some also onto his grey trousers. They made the decision not to contact the Police, but to get rid of the body. At some point the body was moved. Its precise location is difficult to determine; accounts differ slightly, but it seems to have been found nearer to kitchen door than the bottom of the stairs, by the piano, which is where the blood was found.

One of them, probably John, found the mail bag and together they pulled it over Sandra's body. No blue-grey fibres were found on the bag, from which the Police deduced there was no evidence that Lucan had ever touched the sack, let alone placed Sandra's body into it. This was one of the main pieces of evidence which convinced the Police that Lucan had had an accomplice.

He had an accomplice all right. They just didn't recognize her!

Four facts are known. One is that the body had been moved; the next is that the body had been placed in the mail bag; the third is that there were no blue-grey woollen fibres on the bag, or any other evidence that Lucan had ever touched the bag and the fourth that there was a spot of Lady Lucan's blood on the bag, assumed to have been contamination. If one of them held the bag open, and the other pushed the body inside, there may well have been no reason for any fibres from either of their clothing to come into contact with the bag, although a spot of Lady Lucan's blood did.

The body is in the bag. What to do next? Bury it in the garden? Was this when Lord Lucan went briefly into the garden, to assess the possibility of burying the body? Was it he who made those three unidentified, bloody footprints by the garden door? Is that when a few spots of Sandra's blood was transferred from somebody's shoe onto those few leaves in the garden? The garden would soon have been discounted – disturbed earth would have been patently apparent to any investigating officer. It might work for a killer who enticed someone to his house, someone unknown to him and for whom the Police would have no reason to search in that particular garden. But a family member? Bad idea!

The only other option would have been for John to dispose of the body somewhere else. Where? Obviously, somewhere out of town. That would have made it impossible for John to keep his dinner appointment at the Clermont, but some excuse could have been made for that. At that time of night, not yet 9.30 p.m., the chance of being seen if they tried to put the body into the boot of the car straight away were high. It would be better to wait until John left the Clermont.

But there was another problem, which must have become clear to them. Sandra would be known to be missing the next day. They would have to report her disappearance to the Police, who would need to interview Lady Lucan, who would be seen to be carrying severe head injuries. Co-incidence? The Police would think not! Lady Lucan was later to say that she had suggested that Lucan stay for few days until her wounds had healed. She did not say why this idea was rejected, but it would seem to be obvious. The children would miss Sandra and the children would see the injuries.

The intruder theory was the answer. Lucan was to leave; Veronica would tell the Police that an intruder had attacked both Sandra and her. No one would know that Lucan had been in the house at all. Perfect! What went wrong? Lady Lucan was later to say that she never had any intention of abiding by this plan, which she had suggested to lull Lucan into a false sense of security. She always intended to make a run for it as soon as she could. And for once, I believe her.

Having abandoned the idea of disposing of the body in favour of the 'intruder', the next thing should have been to remove Sandra's body from the bag. That never happened. Lady Lucan recounted that she told Lucan she was feeling faint and needed to lie down, so they both went upstairs. According to her account, this took place immediately after Lucan had tried to murder her. He put a towel on the bed and fetched her some water! According to my account, it happened half-an-hour later, around 9.30 p.m. Veronica was quite open in saying that encouraging John to go upstairs to the bedroom was a ruse to allow her time to escape. It is just that she claimed this happened very quickly after the attack. I am suggesting it happened later, when she had realized that the Police would almost certainly reject the 'intruder' theory – no forced entry for one – and that they would quickly draw the conclusion that Sandra had been killed by one of the only two people in the house, and Veronica was determined that it would not be her!

According to Lady Lucan, Lucan went into the bathroom to wash his hands and to fetch a wet cloth for her face. Veronica took the opportunity of the sound of the water from the tap to cover her escape, running down the stairs, out into the street, along the thirty yards to the *Plumbers Arms*, arriving 20 minutes later, or 30 minutes, if you accept her later account.

According to my scenario, after Veronica had rested for a short time, they started to complete their plan. John went into the bathroom, removed his soiled blue-grey sweater, placing it over the towel on the rail. This explains the fibres which were found on the towel. He then put on a brown pullover, which had been hanging in the cupboard, probably used the toilet and washed his hands. This would have taken more time than Veronica's outline, and resulted in more noise from the flushing of water to cover her escape. Lucan took the blue-grey sweater from the towel rail, left the bathroom, expecting to see Veronica lying on the bed. She was gone.

Still clutching the blue-grey sweater, Lucan ran upstairs, calling out 'Veronica, Veronica', bringing Lady Frances out from her bedroom on the floor above. She witnessed her father come out of the Nursery, then run down the stairs and out into the street. The door closed behind him and that was the last she ever saw of him.

Before joining Lord Lucan and leaving No. 46 for the last time, it would be wise to check that the scene we have just left accords with blood group evidence, of which there was plenty.

> Veronica's blood at top of stairs
> Veronica's blood in cloakroom
> Sandra's blood at bottom of stairs
> Veronica's blood on kitchen bench
> Sandra's blood on heel of Veronica's shoe
> Sandra's blood on leaves in garden
> Veronica's blood on bag
> Blood contamination in car from sweater

Veronica always denied she went downstairs to the basement so her blood on the kitchen bench and on the bag was considered 'contamination', as was Sandra's blood on the heel of her shoe. The blood on the few leaves in the garden was unexplained, as was the fact of the door to the garden being unlocked, since there seemed to be no logical reason for the accomplice to go outside. Also unexplained was why there were no 'grey-blue' fibres in either of the pools of Sandra's blood. Susan Maxwell-Scott noticed a damp patch on John's trousers which he explained was there because he had slipped in the blood at the bottom of the stairs. The one place fibres should have been found, according to John's own evidence, and there is no mention of them! He may have slipped, but I do not think he fell. I feel it more likely that he supported Sandra's body on his hip while he and Veronica were placing it into the bag. Such a patch of blood would have been quite large, which would explain why the area was still damp.

What was Lady Lucan thinking? What made her run out of the house when she did? What made her say what she did say to the people at the *Plumbers Arms*? The answers to these questions died when Lady Lucan died. All we can consider is what she did, what she said and the results of those deeds and words. Whether they were what she was intending at the time, we shall never know, but what we do know is that she persisted with the results until the time of her death in 2017.

At the Inquest Lady Lucan stated:

> I ran out of the front door and about thirty yards down the street to the *Plumbers Arms*. From there I was taken to St. George's Hospital.

She gave no information about what she had called out on the way or what she had said to the people gathered at the pub. It must be remembered that the primary purpose of the Inquest was to establish the cause and manner of Sandra Rivett's death. What Lady Lucan did afterwards, was not of immediate interest to the Court. Indeed, it was questioned whether Lady Lucan's testimony should have been allowed at all, since it had no bearing on the attack on Sandra Rivett, which was presumed to have occurred before she came down the stairs and which she had not witnessed. The only evidence relating to the crime under consideration which she was truly able to give was the time. Because Lady Lucan was forbidden by Law to give evidence against her husband, and because it was assumed that any further evidence would be against her husband, even though he had not been charged and was not on trial, no further questions were allowed. It was the landlord of the *Plumbers Arms* who provided the information about what had transpired:

> ... she had cried: "Help me! Help me! I've just escaped from a murderer. He's still in my house. My children, my children."

This is essentially the same as Lady Lucan recalled in the Documentary, the only change being the replacement of the words 'a murderer' by 'being murdered'. What is interesting is not what she said, but what she did not say. Lady Lucan did not say: "My husband is trying to kill me". That, surely, would have been the more natural thing to say if Lord Lucan had, indeed, attacked her? Did Lord Lucan hear any of what she was screaming? Had he run a little way towards the *Plumbers Arms.* A short distance would have been quite natural, I imagine, before he pulled up to think.

If he did hear any of what Veronica was screaming, then he might have thought that perhaps his wife was still sticking to the plan - that she had momentarily become confused when she ran too early - that the thought of running to the *Plumbers Arms* had occurred to her, that it would have slightly delayed the arrival of the Police at the house, giving her husband more time to effect his escape. Maybe she had acted on the impulse without thinking things through. At that time, Lady Lucan was not accusing her husband of being involved in the attack. That came later.

Whatever thoughts were racing through his mind, Lord Lucan knew it was time for him to go! He jumped into the car, flung the blue sweater onto the passenger seat (leaving the blood contamination) and drove off.

I suspect he did not drive far. Indeed, I suspect that he may only have been a street or two away, listening for the arrival of the emergency vehicles. It may not have been until then that he remembered the children. How confused and frightened they would be. It may not have been until then he realized that he needed to find someone to go to the house to take care of the children, who would be frightened and confused by the arrival of the Emergency Services.

It is quite possible that the place where Lucan waited was Chester Square. Chester Square turned off Lower Belgrave Street, just before the *Plumbers Arms*, almost opposite. It just so happened that Lucan knew someone living there, not a close friend, more of an acquaintance, but she was close by.

Madeline Floorman was alone in the house, already in bed, and did not respond to Lucan's frantic ringing of the doorbell. A few minutes later, the phone rang. It was Lord Lucan. She could not understand what he was trying to say. Not receiving the wished for response from Mrs. Floorman, he hung up. Mrs. Flooorman was certain that the call did not come from a call box. Had it done so, she would have heard the 'clunk' of the coins as they dropped when Button A was pressed. It has never been established from where Lucan made this call.

Lucan's next recourse was to contact his mother, the Dowager Countess, who, happily, lived not very far away. This call, also, was believed to have been made from a private line. On first being questioned by the Police, the Dowager had given 'approximately 10.45 p.m.' as the time of the call. At the Inquest, she revised this to 'between 10 p.m.

and 10.30 p.m.'. On the discrepancy being pointed out, the Dowager remained vague, simply insisting that she had been surprised at the lateness of the call, which she had received after returning home from a Labour Party meeting. Since she was reported as having arrived at No. 46 to collect the children at around 10.45 p.m., an earlier time would seem indicated.

No one has ever 'admitted' to being the friend to whom Lucan turned that night for the use of their phone. If the person was a good enough friend, and lived close enough by, why did Lucan not ask that person to go to be with his children? Thompson asked a very pertinent question. Why did Lord Lucan not return to Elizabeth Street to use his own phone? She was unable to provide a completely satisfactory answer to her own question, other than to suggest that Lucan would be expecting the Police to arrive at Elizabeth Street very shortly after discovering the body and he did not want to risk being found there. Against this is the fact that he would have known that he had at least ten minutes, if not more, for the Emergency Services to arrive, grasp the situation, inspect No. 46, find that he was not there and make their way to Elizabeth Street. In fact, they went to the Mews property first, so Lucan would have had plenty of time.

While the exact time at which Lucan banged on Mrs. Floorman's door is not known, I think it can be deduced. We know that Veronica arrived at the Plumbers Arms at 9.45 p.m. That is when Lucan left the house. It would have taken Lucan a minute, at most, to drive to the Floorman's place in Chester Square, had he driven straight there. Had he banged on the door, realized that there was going to be no answer and that he would have to phone, he would have been back in his car by 9.50 p.m. at the very latest. We know that the

Emergency Services still had not been summoned at that time, although he did not know this. What Lucan did know was that there were no sirens to be heard. The obvious thing for him to have done, under those circumstances, would have been to drive home to make the call. Why didn't he?

I believe that Lucan, heart racing, was waiting in his car, possibly in Chester Square, for help to arrive. He knew Sandra was dead. He may not have known about her fall down the stairs. He possibly believed that it was the beating on her head that had killed her. Lady Lucan had received a similar beating. As far as he knew, she was still conscious, but concussion does not always manifest immediately. Swelling on the brain can take time to render its damage. How long it must have seemed to him before the ambulance finally drew up, followed closely by the Police!

What a relief it must have been for Lucan finally to hear those sirens approaching – but not until after 10 o'clock. I believe that, up to that time, he had been thinking only of Veronica. Suddenly, he remembered the children and realized the trauma they were about to experience when the Police entered their house – with no adult present. It was then that he started his frantic knocking on the Floorman's door, at a time which I estimate to have been between 10.05 p.m. and 10.10 p.m. When his urgent knocking did not bring any response, he knew that he would have to try telephoning. He could not go back to Elizabeth Street via Lower Belgrave Square because the Police were there. The extra couple of minutes he spent banging on the door would have been all the time necessary for the Police to arrive.

Then it was that he made his two calls, I believe from a public phone box, courtesy of the operator. I believe the phone call to Mrs. Floorman probably occurred just before

10.15 p.m. and that to his mother not much later.

Naturally, the Police were anxious to speak to the person who had helped Lucan by allowing him to use their telephone, but no one ever came forward to admit to being that friend. The Police checked all the nearby telephone boxes but found no sign of any blood in any of them. That does not surprise me. If Lucan washed his hands so thoroughly that Lady Lucan had time to escape while he was doing so, there is hardly likely to have been any blood on the handset. Even if he had not changed his sweater, there would be no blood on the coin box unless he leant up against it.

So, from where had Lucan made his two calls? The Police dismissed Elizabeth Street because there was no evidence that Lucan had returned there. Ruddick (p. 13) recorded the reaction of Detective Chief Superintendent Roy Ranson, who was the first person to enter Lord Lucan's bedroom at his Elizabeth Street flat. Describing the scene, Ranson said:

> It was so curious. It looked as though it was waiting for its owner to return from the bathroom. On the bed, there was his suit and shirt, and on the bedside table there was his wallet, car keys, change, cheque book and driving licence ... all the things a man usually carries around in his pockets.'

If Lucan had returned to Elizabeth Street to make the phone calls, not only would the Police have expected to have found some evidence of blood, but they would also have expected him to grab some of the things from the bedroom - money, for instance. Yet Luan clearly did not have any money at all with him at the Maxwell-Scott's. He asked Susan to stamp the letters. (Most men carried a book of stamps in their wallet.) The letter to Stoop was posted unfranked.

As to those phone calls, there may be a simple answer.

I worked as a G.P.O. telephonist from 1965-1967. I well remember my very first training session. We were told that, in the very early days, there were no free calls from public telephone boxes, not even in an emergency. Then, one day, someone, who had no money with them, tried to call for an ambulance. The operator refused to connect the call. As a result, someone died. Never again! From then on, emergency calls were free – and that did not necessarily mean only calls to 999. We were told that if there was any sort of emergency and the caller had no money, connect the call, without question. Better that the G.P.O. be cheated out of the cost of a local call than that some disaster should befall as the result of an operator's refusal. If Lord Lucan found a public phone box, explained that his wife had been injured and there was no one to look after his children, that operator would have connected the call, immediately. If the first call was unsuccessful, Lucan would have dialled 'O' for the operator a second time and made the same request of another operator, with the same result. His second call was successful.

Having done all that he could, Lucan left London, probably shortly after 10.15 p.m. The drive to Uckfield from London is, according to Thompson, about one-and-a-half hours. Thompson estimated that, with clearer traffic conditions at night, the drive might have been accomplished in something over an hour. I suggest about an-hour-and-a-quarter. Susan Maxwell-Scott said that Lucan arrived 'around 11.30 p.m.'. If Lucan made the call to his mother at around 10.15 p.m., then arriving at the Maxwell-Scott's home at around 11.30 p.m., sounds about right, give or take five minutes.

When Lucan arrived at Uckfield, he found Ian Maxwell-

Scott had decided to stay in London that night so Susan was home alone, alone, that is, apart from their seven children. Lucan arrived at about 11.30 p.m., and Susan immediately let him in, even though she had already retired for the night. She poured him a scotch and sat down to listen to his tale.

At the inquest, Susan Maxwell-Scott explained that Lucan had not recounted his experiences of that night 'like a story', rather 'it came out in bits and pieces', as it would have if Lucan was trying to meld together the truth with the story which he and Veronica together had agreed to tell. In the documentary, Lady Lucan stated that she did not scream out as she ran down the street, she saved all her breath for running. This is contrary to the evidence of Susan Maxwell-Scott, who stated that Luan told her he had heard her screaming 'Murder! Murder!' This is important, because it may indicate that Lucan was aware that Veronica had not named him as her attacker at that point. He may have been trying to give the 'intruder' story in the hope that this was the story which Veronica was giving to the police. Susan testified that John had told her that Veronica had tried to blame the attack on him, which has the ring of truth.

Veronica was in very genuine distress, hysterical, when Lucan found her. Her first reaction would have been to try to excuse her own behaviour and put the blame on someone else – and who better than he? This is a very basic human reaction. It seems to be born in us. How many parents have ever wondered whether the only two reasons a two-year-old has bothered to learn to speak is (a): to ask for things and (b): to deny culpability? With Veronica's history of accusing him of wanting her dead, what were the chances that she would stick to the 'intruder' story upon which they had agreed, and what were the chances of her simply placing the blame on him?

A 5' 2" female, clearly battered, and a 6' 4" man without a scratch! What chance would he have of saying "It wasn't me! It was her!" and being believed? Somewhere between zilch and zero!

It just so happened that Susan Maxwell-Scott had qualified as a barrister. She had been called to the Bar in 1960 but had never practiced, choosing marriage and the raising of a family over a career. Nevertheless, she would have been of great assistance to Lucan in assessing the situation. If he did not already know, she would probably have explained to him that, under English Law, no wife may testify in Court against her husband. It was not a case of her not being forced to testify. She was not allowed to do so - full stop. Even if Veronica had seen her husband murder Sandra, she could not testify to that effect. The only circumstance under which a wife was allowed to testify against her husband was if she were the victim, if she had been attacked by him.

At first, this might have appeared to be a good thing, but further consideration would have shown John that, if his wife could not take the stand, she could not be cross examined. Under cross-examination, a good defence lawyer should be able to cause her to contradict herself. It would have dawned upon him that, if he were charged first with attempted murder for the attack on her, and if he were to be found guilty, as he almost certainly would be, not only would he be sentenced to a number of years in prison, but if he were then to be charged with Sandra's murder, it would hardly matter if Lady Lucan testified or not. Her story, her version, would already be known.

Ruddick questioned why, in his letter to his brother-in-law, William (Bill) Shand Kydd, written sometime after midnight while at the Maxwell-Scott's house, Lucan wrote:

> ... but am only concerned about the children. If you can manage it, I'd like them to live with you ... For George and Frances to go through life knowing their father had stood in the dock accused of attempted murder would be too much. When they are old enough to understand, explain to them the dream of paranoia, and look after them.

Was 'attempted murder' an error? Had Lucan intended to write 'accomplice to murder? No. He wrote 'attempted murder' because that was the only crime of which Lady Lucan would have been able to accuse him in a Court of Law.

This sad letter contained the first indication that Lucan was not planning to return. Was it a suicide note? Possibly. Many people have thought so, but I cannot believe that, had he had suicide in mind, Lucan would not have written a letter to his children, possibly a short note to each of them, expressing his love and caring. These may have been placed in a separate envelope, for Shand Kydd to give to the children when they were old enough, but I just cannot see Lucan not writing something - anything - directly to his children.

Why no mention of Camilla? I found this very hard to understand but could only conclude that, believing the trial would take place fairly rapidly, he felt that Camilla would still be too young to understand what was happening. The two older children would not only have understood, but so would their 'friends' at school, some of whom might well be quite caustic in their comments. We shall never know.

Lucan then wrote a second letter to Shand Kydd, mostly on business matters, including the upcoming auction of his silver, for which he asked Shand Kydd to oversee the reserve price. (This has been referred to as 'family' silver, but 'family' silver would be 'Trust' and Lucan would not have been able to sell it, surely?)

What had influenced Lucan's decision? Was it only his conversation with Susan? I do not think so. No, I think the turning point was the telephone call he made to his mother, just after midnight. It was brief, but it was overheard at both ends, by Susan Maxwell-Scott at Uckfield and the Police Officer, waiting at the Dowager Countess's home, in case he should make contact there. Lucan asked after the children and was told that they were in bed and to the best of the Dowager's knowledge, asleep. He then asked if Veronica had 'turned up' and was told that she was at the hospital and was going to be all right. There was a short silence. Then the Dowager told Lucan that there was a Police Officer in the room and asked Lucan if he wished to speak to him? Lucan hesitated, but declined.

What is important is not what his Mother said, but what she did not say. She did not say: 'Veronica is going to be all right and she has told the Police all about the intruder'. Lucan would have been digesting the fact that the Police were not just 'wanting to speak to him', but had stationed an officer at the Dowager's house, on an overnight vigil, hoping that he might show up. That could mean only one thing. If not the 'Prime Suspect', he was certainly 'A Person of Interest'!

Would the decision he then made, to disappear, have been any different had he known that the pathologist would find that Sandra had not died as a result of the blows to her head but as a result of suffocation from accumulation of blood in the airways? Possibly not, because he would still be facing definitely one, and most likely two, 'attempted murder' charges, which would not only have brought disgrace on his children, but also have resulted in a lengthy prison sentence.

Lucan would also have known that the only way to defend himself was to implicate his wife - and husbands *were* allowed to testify in Court against their wives!

Time to put his escape plan into effect!

Now we come to the final piece of the puzzle - or should that be two pieces, since it is only by combining information, given by Ruddick early in his book (p. 33) with further information given later, (p. 65) that the picture becomes complete. The last paragraph on p. 33 begins:

> Lucan invested any money he had in jewellery. He said he knew how he was going to leave the country when the revolution came. Jewellery, he said, was portable.

Ruddick continued with an outline of the concerns which Lucan shared with a number of his friends, who seriously anticipated a revolution in England. This may seem outlandish now, but I can assure you that there were very real concerns for the future in post-war Britain. It is hard to explain to people today the intensity of the Cold War. It was not for nothing that Churchill had famously declared that an 'Iron Curtain' had descended across Europe between Russia and the West. The threat of atomic war was very real.

Lucan and I would both have been in London the day the Cuban crisis reached its peak. Incredible as it may now seem, neither Russia nor America then had rockets powerful enough to launch a nuclear attack on the other. America had tried to remedy this problem by building a military base in Turkey. Russia was in the process of responding by building a military base in Cuba. America did not take kindly to this move. There was a thirteen day stand-off, with America giving Russia until 3 p.m. G.M.T. on Thursday, 28th October, 1962, to turn back its supply ship. Britain had declared its support for America and both America and Russia had the capability to launch missiles as far as London. We, in London, assumed the bomb(s), which no one doubted would be nuclear, would fall on us! I remember our office tea lady (and if you don't know what a tea lady was, ask your grandmother!) brought round the tea exactly at three o'clock. With a big smile and a flourish, she placed a cup of tea on each of our desks and said: "Make sure you enjoy this since it is the last cup of tea you will ever have". The boss told me not to bother typing up the material he had just dictated, because there did not seem to be any point, since none of us would be there the next day. We chatted until just before 5 p.m., when the boss said we might as well go home. Hand shakes and "It has been nice knowing you" all round and then out to the bus stop, where I joined the queue of people gazing upwards towards the sky, watching and listening for the approaching aircraft! Six o'clock came and went, so did 7 o'clock and 8 o'clock. Then at 9 o'clock, Big Ben boomed across the nation and the radio announcer said: "This is the BBC Home Service" - the Russians had turned back! That was when I started shaking! (I presume the delay was to allow the Americans to be certain that the Russians had truly turned back. I believe part of the deal was for America to dismantle its base in Turkey, but I am not sure.) It was hectic the next day at the office - all that typing to catch up on!

Ninety-nine years of peace, between 1815 and 1914, had been shattered by the First World War. Since 1914, not only had the German Kaiser fallen from power, so had the hereditary rulers of France, Spain, Italy, Greece; there was hardly a ruling House left in Europe - apart from the United Kingdom. Millions of people had been killed during and following the Russian Revolution - the cruel slaughter of the Russian Royal Family, including the four defenceless princesses, had been particularly brutal. Then there was the

Chinese Cultural Revolution, with the loss of millions more lives. The breakaway of East Pakistan from West Pakistan, when it became Bangladesh, resulted in a bloodbath.

There were problems in Korea, Vietnam, Taiwan, Persia (Iran), Egypt (Suez crisis), Philippines (Marcos family), Papua New Guinea, Cambodia and the Khmer Rouge, plus Africa – troubles in Kenya, Uganda, the Congo, all sorts of places. The worst of the troubles in South Africa were yet to come, but the beautiful country of Rhodesia was in its death throes. The Lucan family had land in Rhodesia and Lucan had a bank account there, the contents of which he could not access owing to International sanctions.

Back home, England was struggling under the leadership of left-wing Prime Minister, Harold Wilson, whom many people considered to be a Russian 'stooge'. The previous year, 1973, there had been great unrest as England reeled under an energy crisis – not just petrol this time, but electricity, with many shops displaying 'No Candles' signs in their windows. In 1973, oil increased in price by 70%. In 1974, inflation was 20%. There had been three budgets that year and there was no sign that things were about to improve.

And then there was Northern Ireland. A quarter of a century after partition, the enmity between Northern Ireland and the remainder of the country was becoming worse, not better. The bombings spread to the mainland and, for the first time, some English Police were armed! The Lucan family were originally from Ireland. They still had an estate there – 60,000 acres – as well as property at Castlebar in County Mayo. If there was any aristocratic family which might be targeted by Irish terrorists, it was the Lucan family. Lord Lucan had good cause to be concerned and was being sensible in making plans to take himself and his family to safety.

Five years later, in 1979, another Irish Earl, Lord Mountbatten, the uncle of Prince Phillip, was murdered by Irish terrorists when they blew up his motor boat. The threat was very real.

For the Upper and more affluent Classes, life in Britain was far from stable. In 1973, the Stock Exchange crashed. There was high taxation (98% on unearned income). The Left-wing Prime Minister, Harold Wilson was thought by many people to be a KGB 'plant' and the Trade Union movement was a constant source of trouble. Markham (p. 122) gave a further account of quite how desperate some people thought the situation in England had become:

> A group called Unison ... was set up by a former deputy director of MI6. It was a vigilante organization, designed to protect the country against a Communist takeover or a general strike. Unison was joined by the ex NATO commander, General Sir Walter Walker, who then formed a group of his own. He claimed to have some 100,000 members, and was openly supported by the Admiral of the Fleet ... Then came Colonel David Stirling, Clermont gambler and founder of the SAS. Stirling formed GB75, a patriotic group that again would act as a private army ... This operation was backed and funded by James Goldsmith ... The private army ... was joined by Dominick Elwes and by Michael Stoop ...

Lucan is not known to have joined any such group, but his position cannot have been made easy by the long-standing affiliation of his mother with Harold Wilson and the Labour Party. You will remember that Lucan's father, the 6th Earl, had been Chief Opposition Whip in the House of Lords when Wilson took over leadership of the Labour Party. Now Wilson was Prime Minister. Lucan dined with his Mother every Sunday evening. Her intense and on-going interest in left-wing politics would have filled one ear with one side of the story while his friends' opposing points of view would have filled the other!

That other piece of the puzzle? That comes with information given by 'the gambler, writer and Greek shipping tycoon Taki Theodoracopoulos' (Ruddick p. 65), friend of Lucan and fellow gambler. Late in the 1970s, he revealed that Lucan had done a number of things in the summer before the murder which, with hindsight, clearly indicated his intention to kill Veronica. Taki did not reveal his source but he was emphatic with his claims. Firstly, Lucan had bought a twenty-foot speedboat, he said, which he kept moored 'on the South Coast'. Secondly, he had made two dummy runs in the car, with a sack in the boot weighing eight stone. Thirdly, Taki recalled coming across Lucan jogging one day in Hyde Park, and this had struck him as odd as Lucan had never before shown any real interest in his physical health.

Taking the third 'revelation' first, Lucan was about to turn forty, no surprise then that he might start to take an interest in his health and fitness! (Remember, when the Police took over Lucan's house in Elizabeth Street as their headquarters, how they made themselves at home, not only using his kitchen, but also his exercise bike?) Marnham (p. 30) records that Lucan "was an officer in the Guards Reserve and he still kept up his pistol practice and his shooting. He had been trained in unarmed combat ...". A jog in the park can hardly be taken as 'evidence' that Lucan was planning a murder!

It is the first two points which are of interest. It appears that Lucan had bought a speedboat - hardly surprising considering his earlier passion for them - but this seems to have been a speedboat of which no one else was aware. That was the whole point of the 'revelation'. Theodoracopoulos only knew that the boat was moored somewhere on the south coast. He assumed that the two runs to the coast with a heavy sack in the boot, apparently weighing 8 stone, were dummy runs to test the time it would take to dump his wife's body in the sea. I am suggesting that the speedboat had been purchased for a 'quick get-away' with his family in the event that a revolution did take place. Items in the sack on each occasion were most likely items of emergency food and drink.

It was to this boat that I believe Lucan made his way after leaving the home of Susan Maxwell-Scott just after 1 a.m. He had declined Susan's offer to stay the night. It would not have been appropriate for him to stay overnight in the house of a married woman when her husband was not present. He had asked her for sleeping pills and had been given four Valium tablets, which I am sure helped him to sleep wherever it was that he pulled the car over. The car was found abandoned in Newhaven. We know that it was abandoned sometime between 5 a.m. and 8 a.m. on the morning of Friday, 8th November, 1974. The man in the house opposite had visited the bathroom at 5 a.m., spent a few moments staring out of the window (doing eye exercises) and was sure that the car was not there at that time. When the gentleman arose again at 8 a.m., there it was!

First light seems an appropriate time for Lucan to have arrived, after having (hopefully) had a few hours' sleep. At some point, using note paper from the glove compartment, Lucan wrote his last letter to his friend, Michael Stoop, the owner of the car, which, being penniless, he was forced to post unfranked. It is quite heart-rending to read:

> ... if you come across my children — which I hope you will — please tell them that you knew me and that all I cared about was them ... I no longer care except that my children should be protected.

Lucan had abandoned all hope, but I still do not believe that he was about to kill himself. If that had been his intention, he would have written something to his children.

In her book, Thompson revealed some very interesting information. Lucan had written, not one, but two letters to Stoop. Because they were unfranked, there was a delay in delivery, delivery not being made until the Monday afternoon, by which time the Corsair had been found. Stoop telephoned the Police, telling them only about one letter. They told him to drop it in when he was passing, which he did at 3.30 a.m. the next morning, without the envelope. This did not please the police, who questioned him as to the post mark and what he had done with the envelope. He insisted that he had thrown it in the bin at the Clermont. They searched the bins, without success. Considering the car had already been found, I am not quite sure what extra information they were hoping to obtain from the envelope.

Stoop never told the Police about the second letter, but he did tell a journalist friend, James Fox, the person who had written the article about Lucan, mentioned earlier. In this letter, Lucan told Stoop where to find the car and that the keys were in the glove compartment. He also asked Stoop to 'forget' he ever lent the car to Lucan and, most importantly, to burn the envelope. Lucan had made no such request of the Maxwell-Scotts.

Why did Lucan not wish the authorities to know that he had been to Newhaven? The obvious answer would seem to be that, if they did, they would know from which Port he had left England. Indeed, they would know that he had left England, which they would not otherwise have done. That would have made tracing him easier. If that was the case, then that would be yet another indication that Lucan was not intending suicide. If he had been, he would not have cared whether they knew or not. Without Veronica's testimony, there was no 'intruder' theory. Sandra could only have been killed by one of two people. At midnight, Lucan had been distressed by the possibility that his children might be forced to witness the spectacle of their father being tried in Court for attempted murder. By dawn, he was forced to face an even more devastating reality. The only way he could clear himself was by accusing his wife. He could not do that – if not for Veronica's sake, then for the sake of his children. He could not force them to witness their mother being tried for murder. Perhaps Veronica could plead insanity? That might be difficult when, only such a short time ago, she had stood before a judge in a Court of Law for a whole two weeks, proving that she was not mentally unfit.

No. There was nothing else for it. Lucan had to disappear.

Newhaven was the closest seaport to London, an obvious mooring place for an escape boat, but it was not the closest seaport to the Continent. The weather was bad that night and, much as I would like to believe that Lucan made his escape and lived a happy life, alas, that untouched Swiss Bank account tells a different story. The 20 ft. speedboat was not built for 'open water'; it was an 'in shore' vehicle. Alone, in this small boat, in stormy seas, I fear that Lord Lucan went down with his boat.

May he rest in peace

Epilogue

On the 3rd February 2016 John, 7th Earl of Lucan, was legally declared dead.: 41 years, 2 months and 26 days after his disappreance.

Lady Lucan died on the 26th September 2017, as a result of an overdose of drugs and alcohol. She is survived by her three children.

The documentary "Lord Lucan, My Husband, The Truth" was finally released on 5th June 2017.

Bibliography

Darwin, Charles. (1859/1998) *The Origin of Species.* Ware, Herts: Wordsworth Editions

Marnham, Patrick. (1988) Trail of Havoc: In the steps of Lord Lucan (2nd edn.) London: Penguin Books

Ruddick, John. (1994) Lord Lucan: What really happened. London: Headline Book Publishing

Thompson, Laura., (2014) A Different Class of Murder: The Story of Lord Lucan. London, Head of Zeus Ltd.

About the Author

Denise Carrington-Smith was born in 1937, the same year as Lady Lucan. She spent her childhood in London, migrating to Australia with her young family in 1967.

Having trained in yoga, which she taught for some years, Denise qualified as a Natural Therapist, specializing in homoeopathy. She lectured in herbalism, Bach Flower Remedies and homoeopathy before establishing the Victorian College of Classical Homoeopathy, of which she was Principal for a number of years. She also served as both State and Federal President of the Australian Federation of Homoeopaths.

Recognizing the need for profressional training in counselling, Denise qualified as a psychologist and also a hypnotherapist.

Denise retired to Far North Queensland at the end of 1995, returning to University, where she took up the study of archaeology, receiving her doctorate in 2013.

Denise has seven children, eighteen grandchildren and a smattering of great-grandchildren.

www.ingramcontent.com/pod-product-compliance
Lightning Source LLC
Chambersburg PA
CBHW070256010526
44107CB00056B/2477